"This is a 'how to' book in the deepest sense. In *A Happy Marriage*, Rebecca winsomely deals with the foundational principles of this most basic of human institutions and their practical implications. The breadth of her historical and cultural context is unique. Her observations are profound."

—Barbara Challies
Widow and mother
Dalton, Ga.

"*A Happy Marriage: Covenant Joy in a Fallen World* is a unique book on marriage. Through the honest reflections of a number of couples, younger and older, and her own biblical/pastoral reflections on God's good gift of marriage to His creatures, Rebecca VanDoodewaard explores, often with an unsettling honesty, the joys, privileges, sorrows, and strains experienced by Christians in marriage. Just as the Bible never allows us to imagine that life in a fallen world will ever be without tears, Rebecca acknowledges this, but shows us that for Christians, marriage is a gracious gift from a God who longs to see His children experience 'covenant joy in a fallen world.' I recommend this book without any hesitation."

—Dr. Ian Hamilton
Professor and cofounder
Westminster Seminary UK

"A happy and holy marriage serves as one of the greatest blessings this life has to offer the Christian pilgrim. Yet few Christian books present these twin gifts of happiness and holiness as ready blessings to be found within the confines of marriage. Rebecca VanDoodewaard has written a book which casts this right vision. Whether couples are just embarking upon this journey, muddling their way through the middle years, or looking at the finish line, here is a book that will encourage, challenge, and comfort. *A Happy Marriage* is a happily realistic book offering a biblical lens with personal and practical applications that any and all marriages will benefit from."

—Rev. Jason and Leah Heloploulos
East Lansing, Mich.

"The marketplace for Christian books on marriage is bulging, so one might wonder if there is room for another one. Yet there is. Such is the breakdown and the watering down of the idea of marriage, not only in the secular world, but sadly also among Christians—we, too, need to be reminded afresh of the richness of this God-ordained gift and blessing. In a way that leans heavily on the rich portrayal of marriage from many angles in the Bible, Rebecca VanDoodewaard walks us through its relevant passages to explore the rich depths of this relationship. Most notably, she points to the intimate connection between marriage as the bond between a man and a woman on earth and the sacred saving union between believers and Christ, their heavenly Bridegroom, and the rich benefits that we find in Him. Here is a volume that will benefit not only those who are preparing for marriage and seeking to understand all that it entails but also those who are already married and need to rediscover afresh the joys and blessings of this unique gift from God."

—Rev. Mark and Fiona Johnston
Bangor, Northern Ireland

"I was once one of Rebecca's pastors, and she would often ask me, 'What books have you read lately?' Now I'm pleased to say, '*A Happy Marriage*, and I loved it!' Such timely but often neglected topics. Such theologically rich reflections confirmed by personal testimonies. Such biblically wise counsel made simple and accessible. The more I read, the more I thought of the couples I counsel. This is gold, and I can't wait to recommend it."

—Dr. Greg Norfleet
Pastor of Counseling
Briarwood Presbyterian Church, Birmingham, Ala.

A Happy Marriage

A Happy Marriage

Covenant Joy in a Fallen World

REBECCA
VANDOODEWAARD

A Happy Marriage: Covenant Joy in a Fallen World

Published by Ligonier Ministries
421 Ligonier Court, Sanford, FL 32771
Ligonier.org

Printed in China
Amity Printing Company
0000725
First edition

ISBN 978-1-64-289711-1 (Hardcover)
ISBN 978-1-64-289712-8 (ePub)

Cover design: Ligonier Creative
Interior design and typeset: Ligonier Editorial

Library of Congress Control Number: 2024952043

For Bill, with whom I have been very happy.

Contents

"Marriage, which has been the bourne of so many narratives, is still a great beginning, as it was to Adam and Eve, who kept their honeymoon in Eden, but had their first little one among the thorns and thistles of the wilderness. It is still the beginning of the home epic—the gradual conquest or irremediable loss of that complete union which makes the advancing years a climax, and age the harvest of sweet memories in communion."

—George Eliot, *Middlemarch*, 1872

"Almighty God, who at the beginning did create our first parents Adam and Eve, and did sanctify and join them together in marriage: Pour out upon you the riches of his grace, sanctify, and bless you, that ye may please him both in body and soul; and live together in holy love until your lives' end."

—The Book of Common Prayer, 1521

Introduction

Christian marriage is important because it is a declaration of true, ultimate love in a world that is hungry for true and ultimate love. It points sinners to salvation through Jesus' substitutionary, loving sacrifice and leadership. It points to eternity, where marriage itself will no longer be needed because communion will be fulfilled. History's metanarrative is a love story, and it has a heavenly ending.

We know this on a gut level. This is why happy endings in books and films are satisfying. This is why, in a broken world, we still look for true love and get married. But it seems that the longer you look around, the more complex marriage looks. The fairy tales of childhood all end "happily ever after"; it is easy to believe them until your castle in the air is blown away by adultery or violence or abandonment in a marriage that you have seen or experienced. Since the garden of Eden, Satan has been attacking God's plan for marriage. As the initiation of the world's fundamental social structure as well as a picture of redemption, God's best earthly gift is a target. The devil has used different tactics through history, but he has never let up in his assaults, from Eden on, often capitalizing on our own sin. Our world is full of unhappy and broken marriages. It is loaded with misrepresentations of Christ's relationship to His church. And so it is easy to be jaded, resigning ourselves to the fact that "happily ever after" is only for a storybook princess.

But though the fall into sin damages every marriage—some irreparably—God's good design for marriage is still here. He has given this beautiful, created ordinance, and "best are all things as the will / Of God ordained them; his creating hand / Nothing imperfect or deficient left / Of all that he created."[1] We still have God's original good pattern, design, and promise to bless His people. Regardless of our personal experience, there is an intended experience of marriage. The ideal still exists because Christ is still committed to His church, His bride, His people. God has designed marriage for great blessing, and so we can expect that. When two Christians make a lifelong commitment to each other, they are effectively and demonstrably declaring that they trust God's plan for marriage and trust that He will use it for His designed purpose. Marriage is bigger than our happiness, but God designed happiness to go with marriage. When, by grace, we live in a relationship that accords with God's design for His glory, we can expect the joy that He designed to accompany it.

This expectation cannot be rooted in other people, though. If we look to other sinners to fulfill us and be the basis for happiness, we will be unfulfilled. Jane Austen commented that marriage is the relationship "in which people expect most from others and are least honest themselves."[2] Other people will disappoint us; we will disappoint other people. The closer we are to someone, the more often this is true. But God never disappoints, and because His design is "very good" and for the Christian's good, because He is working all things together for our good and promises to bless Christian marriage, we can expect happiness from Him as we follow His plan.

Notice that this is biblical, not "traditional," marriage. Traditions change from era to era, from culture to culture. People start new traditions and update old ones. There is nothing wrong with that, because traditions are often expressions of human creativity and—like stockings above a fireplace, red envelopes at Lunar New Year, or bonfires on November 5—they add legitimate fun to life. We can change traditions, add to them, or even leave them out of our lives with no real consequence.

Marriage is not a tradition. Marriage, as given by God in His Word, just *is*, whether we like it or not, whether it is part of our cultural background or not. Biblical marriage is part of the Lord's creation, like Everest or the moon. A shift in tradition does nothing to change it. Noncompliance, though it will change our experience, has no effect on it. Emotions will not affect its existence. And because God created it to bless us, we can enjoy it instead of fight, deny, or reshape it.

But why is happiness in marriage even important? If we are being faithful to each other and doing our work, is happiness just icing on the cake? No. If marriage is supposed to be a picture of Christ and the church, then a relationship that is generally unhappy or bland is a misrepresentation. Having a happy marriage is not first about our avoiding misery, though that is one inevitable result. Just as God does not exist for our happiness, neither does His design of marriage. But just as we find greatest happiness and greatest blessing in knowing God, so we find great happiness and blessing in following His design for our closest human relationship. All true happiness—all blessing—is a byproduct of something more magnificent: knowing God and being remade in the image of His Son. Obedience to Him as part of our reasonable worship will bring blessing, just as certainly as sin and rebellion will bring misery. Through Scripture, salvation is communicated in terms of joy: God has promised that His people will ultimately be eternally happy in Him even as He rejoices over them (e.g., 1 Sam. 2:1; Pss. 119:162; 126; 132:16; Isa. 35:10; 65:14, 18–19; Rev. 19:7).

Happiness in marriage is also about accurately showing—to each other, to children, to church, and to community—the church's joy in her union with Christ. The church's destiny is happiness: "Joy and gladness will be found in her, thanksgiving and the voice of song" (Isa. 51:3). A faithful marriage that is happy is a clearer, truer picture than a marriage that is simply faithful. That does not diminish faithfulness: it elevates happiness. And rightly so: God Himself repeatedly uses the joy of a happy marriage to picture His own love for His people. Isaiah 62 is a well-known illustration: "For as a young man marries a young woman, so shall your sons marry you, and as the bridegroom rejoices over the bride, so shall your God rejoice over you" (v. 5).

Contemporary Western culture says that our happiness is essential—absolutely primary. It treats faithfulness as optional or even opposed to happiness. Happiness is to be pursued at nearly any cost by any means. Sadly, confessionally faithful churches often behave the opposite way, as though faithfulness were primary, with marital joy as a bonus. One wedding liturgy still in use actually begins: "Whereas married persons are generally, by reason of sin, subject to many troubles and afflictions, to the end that you . . . may also be assured in your hearts of the certain assistance of God in your affliction."[3] The expectation is fidelity despite misery, not fidelity fed by joy.

Emphasizing either faithfulness or happiness to the detriment of the other is a distorted picture of the relationship between Christ and His church (Eph. 5). They are not mutually exclusive. In fact, they are intimately connected. Faithfulness is essential: so is happiness.

Both will take work. Happiness, as more abstract, might take deeper thought and conversation. It might take more emotional effort and understanding. But these are the warp and woof of a healthy gospel union, byproducts of loving and following our Creator. An unhappy marriage can be functional at one level. It can be faithful. A happy marriage, though, is the most accurate picture of healthy Christian faith in Jesus. It will also be a marriage in which faithfulness flourishes.

But this happiness is not without context. Feeling "happy" with no context or boundaries for the happiness can lead to distortion and spiritual death. Some marriages are happy that should not be. Look at Ahab and Jezebel: they helped each other reach goals and fulfill dreams. They supported each other and shared ambitions, working together toward perceived success (1 Kings 21:1–16). Things were probably pretty harmonious in the palace in Samaria. Partnering together for an evil goal can bring union and fleeting happiness. Ananias and Sapphira had no discord when they decided to lie about their donation to the church (Acts 5:1–11). Both of these couples had a unity that showed its distortion in the death and misery that it spawned. When happiness in marriage is an end in itself or is a means to sin, then it is not a worthy goal. Happiness should be part of Christian marriage not only for our blessing, but as the most accurate advertisement of the love and joy demonstrated in God's work of salvation. It is a reflection of our happy submission to Jesus' lordship. If happiness is not there within this context, then we have a problem.

Neither is happiness without definition. It is sometimes difficult to touch on what it is, though, or to identify happiness. Personality and culture will affect the expression of relational happiness. Circumstances will change our experience of it. Time will change its tempo. Robert Browning wrote about the happiness in his marriage as being like a spider's web: something that can't always be seen and that breaks when touched. "Help me to hold it!" he tells his wife, Elizabeth: "Silence and passion, joy and peace."[4] Silence and passion might be a personal experience, but joy and peace are biblical ideas that all happy Christian marriages share. Different marriages will experience it in different ways and to different degrees at times, but for a Christian marriage, blessing—including happiness—should be present to some extent. It develops and deepens over time, often in fits and starts. But when, by faith, we walk in God's design for marriage with another believer to God's glory, can we expect Him to withhold His promised blessing?

We can expect this when we understand that we do not define *happy*. We do not have the knowledge or the power to do so. God is the One who does, and we see His definition in Scripture as it links happiness with holiness—with God's blessing. The word sometimes translated "happy" in the English Standard Version can also be translated as "blessed" (Gen. 30:13; Eccl. 10:17; Isa. 32:20, KJV). It is tied primarily with the blessing of relationship with God, but also with the covenant community. Yet this happiness is not a stoic, positive knowledge: there is deep emotion here. The blessing of relationship with God and another saved human should bring emotional life to us. In other translations, the word translated "happy" in the ESV is substituted with "cheer up" (Deut. 24:5, KJV) and even "making merry" (1 Kings 4:20, KJV).

The Old Testament speaks many times of happiness, and regularly associates covenantal union with joy. In one place, it commands it: "Let your fountain be blessed, and rejoice in the wife of your youth. . . . Be intoxicated always in her love." (Prov. 5:18–19).

Biblically, happiness is living under God's covenant favor and not His displeasure. It is enjoying His blessing, having been redeemed from the curse of the fall and sin. It is living according to His Word.

Scripture assumes that there should be happiness in marriage. Adam and Eve, especially before the fall (Gen. 2:23), Isaac and Rebekah (24:67; 26:8), Ruth and Boaz (Ruth 4), and many other couples through the Bible show their enjoyment of God's great gift of marriage as they find happiness, comfort, and fun in each other's love. Anonymous couples also play a role, particularly in Psalm 45 and the Song of Solomon. Individual anonymity allows the focus to be on the happiness of union—the joy of two becoming one in covenantal bonds.

God uses the familiar joy of marriage as a picture that we know and experience to help us understand His joy in His people. This is not limited to Ephesians chapter 5, which contains the most explicit connections between marriage and salvation. God also uses this analogy from the Old Testament right through to Revelation (e.g., Isa. 62:4–5; Jer. 2:2; Matt. 9:15; Rev. 21:2). The places where Scripture speaks of a lack of wedded joy and faithfulness are places of darkness and judgment (e.g., Ezek. 16; Hos. 4:14). God Himself connects marriage with happiness and blessing and uses that familiar blessing to help us understand the joy of salvation. Martyn Lloyd-Jones wrote that "the picture is of our Lord rejoicing in the relationship, happy in it, triumphant in it, glorying in it."[5] This salvation is the root of all lasting marital happiness. It is the source.

But real happiness does not exclude sadness, hardship, or suffering in a marriage. Our own sin and sheer fallenness are the biggest obstacle to relational joy. Sin in ourselves and our spouses conspires against happiness. So do the fallen world and the devil. Just as the church walks through this pilgrim journey often feeling the thorns and thistles, so most (if not all) marriages go through valleys and dark places. A relationship can still be happy without being all roses and sunshine. Blessedness can coexist with grief, past or present. "In happiness," Augustine wrote, "I remember past sadness, and in sadness I remember past happiness."[6] Life is complex. Circumstances can change and influence, but they do not dictate. A couple can grow closer together while walking through situations that threaten and press in. A happy marriage is not the fruit of pleasant circumstances: a couple can have a miserable relationship in comfortable, easy surroundings, as Hollywood gives us daily proof. Happiness might not look like bliss or ease, and it can experience growth even in a hostile environment.

This book attempts to examine happiness and marriage with this in mind. Many marriage books warn, diagnose issues, and troubleshoot. Many prescribe advice without nuance for temperament and situation. Too often, authors write about their own marriages, with understanding or advice coming out of individual experience: what works for them becomes a principle that will benefit any marriage, instead of a practice that has been useful in their own circumstances. Even Christian authors often normalize mediocrity and struggle in marriage, arguing that because we are broken, we cannot expect too much from the relationship, placing a burden of unbiblical categories on couples, instead of recognizing and embracing the Lord's good gift. Few marriage books try to think through the joy inherent in God's design, darkness notwithstanding. But this is what Christian marriages and the surrounding culture need—to see the beauty and glory intrinsic to the closest of human relationships. Because behavior flows from thought and belief, a Christian marriage will be healthiest when the spouses are thinking biblically.

We have a Creator who loves not only creation but especially His children. The whole system that He gives us is meant for our gladness. Marriage is part of the original design that is "very good." When we fail to consider the design, we fail to truly understand and utilize the thing itself. The more complex something is, the more true this is: you might not read the instructions on the blender box, but you will likely find out all about your sports car so that you can better enjoy and care for it. We fail to consider God's design of marriage to our own hurt and mediocrity. Marriage has not evolved over the span of human existence to make societies functional. It is not random. It is not something that we can safely play around with, taking out design elements that we don't like or understand, and plugging in our own parts. Instead, marriage is something to cherish as a gift from a loving, omniscient Creator. It is something—like a great work of engineering or art—to ponder and admire and gratefully use as well as enjoy. This book tries to help in that direction.

To try to show the beauty of God's design, I have asked several couples about their happy marriages. These people represent multiple countries and many cultures. They are doctors and students and factory workers and retired folks. They are multilingual and monolingual, childless and quiverfull, urban and rural, settled and sojourning, joyful and grieving. All of them profess faith in the Lord Jesus and are living out that faith in marriages that seek to accurately reflect Christ's love where they are, serving their families and local congregations. These couples have kindly shared their stories as a means of thinking through happiness in different relational contexts and challenges. The last story is not an interview, but a widow's thoughts from the perspective of two completed marriages. With one exception I have arranged the interviews by length of marriage, in order to give a picture of the sorts of progression that a Christian marriage can make over time. They also show that God does and will bless His children, even through darkness. A blessed marriage comes not from chasing happiness, but by seeing the happiness of glorifying and enjoying God together, embracing the gift of marriage that God has put in front of us in His design for our blessing. The couples represented here are living examples of this.

In between their stories, I have sought to identify built-in aspects of marriage that facilitate happiness. It is not a comprehensive list—no doubt others could add facets. But these seemed fundamental, though often overlooked or overshadowed. Other aspects, such as communication, I allude to, but they are so regularly discussed elsewhere that it seemed redundant to include them here.

Our culture not only treats marriage lightly but is also dismissive of biblical marriage as narrow and repressive. Like all fallen cultures, it has exchanged God's truth about marriage for a lie. I hope the stories in this book show the truth about fulfillment and peace and happiness that obedience brings. Sin and grief touch every aspect of our relationships—some more, some less. But there is nowhere that sin and grief go that grace cannot. No corner of a Christian marriage is out of reach. Happiness thrives when we understand the sufficiency of Christ. God has designed marriage for great blessing: we can actually enjoy it throughout this life.

There is something important to note, though: this book is written to Christians. Anyone may read it, but unless you are trusting in Christ for the forgiveness of your sins, unless your life is centered on worship of the God who made, saved, sanctifies, and has promised to glorify you, you will find much here puzzling. Because marriage is a picture of Christ and the church, you cannot fully or properly understand it until you come to know the God who created it—and you. When that happens, it will become clear that while marriage is for us, it is not about us. It will also mean that the atmosphere of a marriage will flow out of our identity in Christ. It will come from who we are, not what we do. It will come from strong roots and not be borrowed fruit. If what we do is not coming out of who we are in Christ, it will be unsustainable at best, deceptive at worst. Sanctification by the Spirit makes holiness—and real happiness—possible. Christians are made increasingly holy by the Spirit, and this is why we have hope, not only for happiness in a marriage, but ultimately in God Himself. If you are not a believer, my hope is that you find the living water that can sustain you through this life and give you the happiness of fellowship with God Himself.

This book is not written only for married people. That is simply because God did not create marriage only for married people. It affects all of us, as children, siblings, friends, and members of society. The happiness of the marriages around us will certainly affect our own lives and joy. The stability of a community partly depends on the stability of publicly committed relationships, and if marriages begin to crumble or spread lies and unhappiness, it changes things for everyone. The reverse is also true, which is why all of us—single, married, divorced, or widowed—need to be thinking biblically and carefully about marriage. When we do, we can appreciate, protect, and encourage the relationships around us, regardless of our own marital status. We can value this gift of God to humanity.

Abuse, abandonment, infidelity, and divorce are topics beyond the scope of this book. But please know that if you are in an unhappy marriage, there is hope and there is help. If you are in an unsafe marriage, the same is true. God values His children even more than He values His temporal institution of marriage: marriages that misrepresent Christ's sacrificial love must be dealt with. The stakes are too high for silence. Marriage was made for people, not people for marriage. Call your family, go to a friend, talk with a safe pastor, involve the police. Do whatever you need to do in order to protect yourself, any children, and the community from a marriage that spreads lies and misery.

My thanks go to the many couples and widow who opened their lives so that we could learn from their stories. They responded with grace and generosity to a request that asked something very personal of them. I am truly grateful for their kindness, time, and wisdom. Their lives are evidence of things not seen.

The staff at Ligonier were kindly professional throughout the writing and publishing process. Barry York patiently answered Greek queries. Matt Kingswood read through the manuscript with the eyes of a theologian, the heart of a pastor, and the kindness of an uncle. Although she finished educating me decades ago, my mother continues to teach me through her wisdom, which she gave to various drafts when I asked. My children were patient about another book project, and my husband never flagged in his encouragement and support.

1

Exclusivity

I am my beloved's, and his desire is for me.
—Song of Solomon 7:10

Deciding to get married can be daunting not only because we do not fully know the other person, but also because marriage is for life. This one person will shape our future, children, financial condition, health, and reputation more than any other human. It can be an intimidating thought! We understand Jane Austen's Elinor Dashwood as she works through that feeling: "It is bewitching in the idea of a single and constant attachment, . . . one's happiness depending entirely on any particular person."[1] One person for life does not always seem reasonable.

Perhaps this is partly why our culture does not believe that lifelong monogamy is possible, let alone happy. It pushes exclusive offers, exclusive vacations, exclusive experiences. These things are not only welcomed but also eagerly pursued. Exclusive relationships are not. They are seen as quaint or repressive, and certainly not morally mandatory. Without a Christian worldview, this would be reasonable.

Voluntary commitment to another human through things that you cannot see or anticipate is foolish, unless this is part of the way that marriage was designed. And it is. Because marriage is a picture of Christ and the church, exclusivity is actually an aspect that both the type and the archetype share. The exclusivity of marriage reflects the exclusivity of the gospel.

This design aspect is clear from the garden of Eden on, as Scripture shows in precept and story the blessing of covenantal monogamy and the misery that comes when we toy with God's design. Because the design is so clear, the exclusivity of marriage is dissolvable only in the face of stark covenantal violation (Jer. 3:8; Matt. 5:32).

But there are exclusive marriages that are unhappy. Such relationships are an aberration from the created norm. The misery does not come from the exclusivity, as our culture so often argues, but is—like all other unhappiness—ultimately a result of sin. It is the unhappiness of exclusivity without God's blessing.

Emotional and sexual exclusivity in marriage is not only the ideal; it should be the expectation, certainly for believers. When couples stick with each other "for better, for worse, for richer, for poorer, in sickness and in health," they create structure for society. They create stability, predictability, and coherence for each other and those around them. Children can grow up with the conviction that their parents will always be together. Faithfully married couples tend to be stronger financially, not only in terms of accumulated wealth but also in terms of financial stability, literally enriching society.[2] Married people tend to be healthier—this is especially true for men—with lower rates of chronic disease, and serious illness diagnosed more quickly.[3]

But of course, God is not only concerned with practicalities; He designed the exclusivity of lifelong, monogamous marriage for our happiness as well, even apart from lower blood pressure and stronger retirement funds. A marriage covenant and marital contentment join to facilitate exclusivity and the happiness designed to flow from it. "A covenant relation," J.I. Packer explains, "is one in which two parties are permanently pledged to each other in mutual service and dependence."[4] The assurance of one other human being always willing to help, comfort, and support you, as you are ready to do the same for that person, brings blessing.

In the summer of 1922, Lord Louis Mountbatten married Edwina Ashley.[5] He had education, military experience, and blood connections to most of Europe's royal families. She had inherited an incredible fortune from her grandfather, making her one of the wealthiest women in Britain. Both were young, good-looking, and apparently in love. Their wedding was the social event of the decade. Not long into their marriage, however, Edwina began a long-term affair with a man who would be by her side for years. But she did not limit herself to him: it was publicly known that she was promiscuous, and for many years, public sympathy was with her husband as he simply bore with it. The strange thing is, when Louis eventually committed adultery himself, Edwina was devastated. Their younger daughter wrote: "My mother found it impossible not to be jealous. The fact that she had been taking lovers for ten years was apparently of no account."[6] Blind or hardened to her own sin, Lady Mountbatten could still see the wrongness of her husband's unfaithfulness to her. Even in a marriage that was already broken, new unfaithfulness brought new grief.

The broken Mountbatten marriage clearly pictures what we see in the marriages around us that have been damaged or destroyed by infidelity. It shows the unhappiness that discontentment and broken covenants bring: the fractured unity, the inability to trust, the disregard of personhood, crippled fruitfulness, and so many other implications, seen and felt.

No matter how we like to suppress it, the exclusivity of marriage's design permeates reality. We actually want it, don't we? Perhaps not in our current situation, but everyone welcomes commitment and devotion in a lover. It takes a very hardened heart to turn away from a spouse who is eager to be with you for the long haul, through thick or thin, and make you the one special person in life regardless of what that life holds. We crave this—a deep, unifying, whole-person friendship with someone who is all ours. This is why novels and films are able to use such a narrative to make money and why fairy tales endure through centuries.

This is because a lack of full commitment brings a host of issues. A spouse not committed to an emotionally and sexually exclusive relationship with his or her marriage partner leaves the partner exposed. This can happen emotionally as confidential thoughts and feelings and habits are shared conversationally with others, shutting down communication within a marriage as spouses instinctively self-protect. Or maybe it is social flirtation that simply leads to suspicion and coolness.

A loss of sexual exclusivity inevitably involves comparison, bringing distrust and insecurity to the marriage bed. When there is no exclusivity, uncertainty of all kinds creeps in: *Where is my spouse? What is he doing? Does she really love me? Why does he feel the need for fulfillment in other people? Am I doing something wrong?* Feelings of inadequacy for the betrayed spouse are almost always part of the situation. One young woman, realizing that her husband was having an affair with a secretary, was blunt about the questions that haunted her: "Is she blonde? Thinner than I am? With bigger breasts?" Infidelity—via bed or screen—kills the happiness that God designed to accompany exclusivity.

Exclusivity is compromised by more than actual adultery, though. Perhaps we are so immersed in our culture's norms that we cannot see the damage that our entertainment choices do to the happiness in our relationships. In the fourth century AD, living in a large, cosmopolitan city, John Chrysostom saw the entertainment industry of his day as opposing happiness in marriage by making light of immodesty, sexual sin, and exclusivity. People "laugh and are pleased, applauding in [the show] what they ought to stone them for." These people "profanely exhibit the sacred things of marriage, and make an open mock of the great mystery."[7] Happiness does not thrive in relationships that feed on such things. If it was true in the 380s, it is even truer now, when entertainment has become ubiquitous, is often free, and has its immorality heightened by technology.

The inverse of all these is part of the happiness that God has inseparably connected to exclusivity. Relational exclusivity brings the joy of being free and safely vulnerable to one person devoted to you, who wants to spend his or her life getting to know you better and love you more deeply. It is the happiness of being the apple of somebody's eye, above everyone else.

Sexual exclusivity is a physical expression of this devotion—a corporeal presence that says, "I'm all yours." It is the freedom of vulnerability and joy in a place where no one else may go. The physical desire for each other is an outworking of whole-person exclusivity. When it is absent or twisted, so is the joy that it is designed to bring. The distortion of self-centered sex will bring only a distorted and fleeting pleasure, not real joy. In contrast, exclusive, other-focused intimacy ushers blessing into a relationship.

Emotional exclusivity is also a gift that strengthens and brings joy to a marriage. In our culture, this is perhaps even rarer than sexual exclusivity. When we are bound to our spouses in covenant, there should be things that we share only with them, from past experiences to certain opinions to inside jokes. And while emotional exclusivity certainly precludes romantic relationships with people other than our spouses, as well as deeply personal friendships that could lead to adultery, our culture has taken its assault on emotional exclusivity to another level with social media. Sharing our emotions and histories and hopes binds us to other people. It is supposed to, so that our relationships can deepen in meaning and closeness. But in a world that rewards sharing on very public platforms, these bonds weaken as they stretch to include thousands of "friends" and "followers." Very little is sacred. Very little is off-limits. Very little is emotionally exclusive to our marriages. And even things that seem admirable, such as posting about how much we love a spouse, expose intimacy to public scrutiny—putting our closest relationship on emotional parade. The extent of the privacy in a healthy marriage will vary from couple to couple, based on personality, circumstances, and other elements, but it needs to be there. Emotional exclusivity involves protecting the privacy of a relationship, partly by not broadcasting details of our emotions, histories, and hopes, but reserving the deepest things about ourselves for the person closest to us. It means sharing in proportion to physical and relational closeness.

And this will bring the blessing that God designed to go with it. The joy of an emotional exclusivity can be beautifully seen in things such as a handwritten note instead of a "best husband ever" post.

It is refusing to share about the inner workings of your marriage when everyone else in the conversation is, and sitting down with your spouse at the end of the evening with a clear conscience and the opportunity for an intimate talk. There is real blessing there; exclusivity promotes unity.

In a relationship that is to be a picture of Christ and the church, exclusivity not only brings happiness but also shows how essential faithfulness is to that joy. Scripture uses adultery as an allegory for idolatry—spiritual adultery. Isaiah, Jeremiah, and perhaps especially Hosea are full of stories and accounts of Israel's whoring after other gods and losing the blessing that came with covenantal exclusivity. There is no real happiness in prostitution: none but Zion's children know solid joys and lasting pleasures (Ps. 16:11).[8] Scripture points this out to warn us and bless us.

The personified inverse of this Old Testament illustration might be the Samaritan woman at the well (John 4). Her past is full of men: some have perhaps taken advantage of her, or perhaps she has taken advantage of them. Either way, she has been looking for satisfaction and happiness but has been unable to find it because she is working against the way that God wired the world. The shame is real, coming from both her community and her conscience. She tries to turn the conversation with Christ away from her colored past. She has come to the well to get water but gets the Man who is the answer to her fundamental need. Her search for satisfaction comes to an end with spiritual happiness and exclusivity. She recognizes this and literally runs to tell others about it. She understands that, like a real marriage, spiritual commitment is a whole-person thing. She has moved—been moved—from promiscuity to faithfulness because of her conversion. It is what Thomas Chalmers called "the expulsive power of a new affection."[9] It will certainly affect her sex life, but the joy-filled transformation is much bigger than one aspect—the exclusivity of a new and ultimate affection and its attendant power. If Jesus did not love His Bride, then exclusivity would be irrelevant. Because He does, exclusivity is crucial.

The joy of exclusivity in a Christian marriage is a symptom and outworking of spiritual fidelity—a relational manifestation of a theological reality. When life is Other-focused, we are able to give ourselves away. This is why happiness in marriage, as well as in spiritual life, is tied to a dying to self. Sinclair Ferguson observes that the Christian life "is an all-or-nothing thing. In trusting [Christ], you will lose your life, but at the same time, you will find it. You must die to self to find yourself. And then you will be set free from the self-love that has crippled your life."[10] As long as life is about us, we will be spiritually and relationally disabled to the extent that we are turned in on ourselves.

Any dying, including dying to self, is an uncomfortable thing. But the pain of putting the old man to death does bring happiness because freedom from self always does. Albert Einstein spoke about the necessity of "a far-reaching emancipation from the shackles of personal hopes and desires."[11] Looking at ourselves brings unhappiness because we cannot manufacture happiness on our own. Like salvation, it is outside ourselves—*extra nos*. Emancipation from preoccupation with self enables us to realistically enjoy marriage and the exclusivity that God wove into it. Self-obsession is not a friend to exclusivity—or happiness. Ben Franklin quipped, "He that falls in love with himself will have no rivals."[12] Ironically, an obsession with self is often a significant factor in abandoning exclusivity and the accompanying blessing. "A life of self-renouncing love" is not only "one of liberty" but is also the happiness of loving another well and truly.[13] This is a joy that grows with sanctification and brings real blessing to both spouses in an exclusive marriage.

In addition to freedom from self, exclusivity is linked with contentment. Not the sort of attitude that says, "I suppose I have to be satisfied with what I have, since I can't do any better." That is not contentment; that is resignation. Biblical contentment in a marriage says, "This gift from God is so good, I want to treasure and value and enjoy it for my whole life." It is a happy satisfaction that brings blessing.

In Jane Austen's novel *Mansfield Park*, Henry Crawford is addicted to attracting women, feeding his ego through romantic conquests. While he brings misery to many around him, he ultimately destroys himself: "Could he have been satisfied with the conquest of one amiable woman's affections, . . . there would have been every probability of success and felicity for him."[14] Relational contentment leading to success and felicity: two things that God did design to go with a marriage that is in Christ.

This is why marriage is a covenant: loving-kindness that involves a commitment. Does a young couple at their wedding really understand the implications of "to have and to hold from this day forward, for better, for worse, for richer, for poorer, in sickness and in health, forsaking all others"? They really do not at that point, and even so, at the front of the church they "are looking each other in the eye and they are promising to be there for each other in a future that they do not know and cannot control."[15] Life will change, and unless there is a violation that meets Scripture's requirements for divorce, a marriage must continue. This is why we place social and legal safeguards around marriage. We sometimes need reminders that we did commit to this one other person, promising to study and support him or her for a lifetime—and even that is too short a time to devote to another human being made in God's image.

After a long, faithful, and very happy marriage, a widow told me that the hardest thing about widowhood was not simple loneliness—she had siblings, children, grandchildren, and great-grandchildren, a loving congregation. The hardest thing was that she was no longer the light of another person's life. Nobody who thought that she lit up the room, who was willing to wait for her while she shopped, who filled her car with gas, who wanted to tell her little things and listen to her, who told her that she was beautiful and meant it—even in her late eighties. Her grief was the sadness of losing *the* exclusive human relationship in her life. Perhaps such a loss is true aloneness, but it highlights the beauty of an exclusive relationship that had given joy for decades, not just to the couple, but to everyone around them. The beauty of devotion is powerful. One of the sad things about our culture is that exclusivity is so uncommon that we rarely see it or the beauty that it begets through the years. So one more happiness that comes with exclusivity is the blessing of showing a broken world the joy of faithfulness. John Milton put this delight into Adam's mouth: "Sole Eve, Associate sole, to me beyond / Compare above all living Creatures deare."[16] A marriage bound by biblical exclusivity will sing.

Exclusivity is not primarily about being limited to one, not a posture of being denied something. Instead, it is being freed to something—free to focus on and be close to one other human in a way that makes deep friendship inevitable and formative. It is the happiness of having made a choice and of taking the time and freedom to enjoy it. It is being set apart from the lie of promiscuity to the blessing of covenant promise. It is the happiness of receiving God's good gift. Jim Elliot must have felt this when he wrote of his fiancée, Elisabeth: "Pure grace from Him gave her. . . . Never let it get stale, Lord, I want this woman to be the woman of all women for me."[17]

Story (2016)

Shiva and Gulika first met online in 2010; Shiva was friends with Gulika's brother. Their online interaction continued until February 2016, when they met in person. The same year, they were married. They live in India, where Shiva teaches.

Do you have a happy marriage?

Yes.

How do you know that?

We have three steps to recognize whether we have a happy marriage. First, our love for the Lord makes us prioritize God in our marriage. Second, we are content with each other in Christ as we continue to mature in the gospel of grace. Third, our involvement in family and church life helps us to measure our growth and happiness in marriage.

What makes your marriage happy?

Christ, through whom God loves us and gave us spiritual blessings. The gospel reminds of Christ's love for sinners like us and the grace that redeems. Family, also the church, and ministry in the church and school.

Has it always been happy?

Most of the time, we have been happy. But there were times we were upset and angry.

How did it get to where it is now?

As we are maturing in our understanding of the gospel and marriage, we are becoming happier.

What things have you found that detract from happiness in your marriage?

When one is too busy with work, when one of us is unable to give time to our partner, and when both are strong-willed or opinionated.

How do you deal with remaining sin in yourselves in marriage?

Confessing and forgiving; not dragging in sin and past incidents. Also seeking help from our spouse and a godly mentor, and encouraging accountability to our spouse and mentor.

Are there any habits or patterns that establish or perpetuate happiness?

Time for each other. Understanding and giving up one's opinion in the light of biblical reason. Considering our spouse's desires and needs. Encouraging each other in daily life, vocation, gym/exercise, and ministry in the church. Doing the shopping together. Gardening together.

Who are your marriage role models? Why?

A seminary professor and his wife, because of their family life: love for one another, children, church, and hospitality.

Can you share one story or event that shaped/shifted your relationship, or made you think differently about it or your spouse?

One time, our discussion resulted in a verbal spat, which led me [Shiva] to ask Gulika: "Why am I tolerating you? I should think of divorcing you." She responded: "What are you waiting for? Go ahead." But after thirty minutes, we sought each other's forgiveness not only for the spat, but particularly for "divorce talk." Such a dramatic event has not taken place since then.

In this event, we both assumed that our theological (Pentecostal and Presbyterian) and cultural backgrounds were clashing, which fired up the situation. Thankfully, it was later corrected from a biblical perspective.

How do you live with the sadness of infertility in a good marriage?

Though we do not have children after years of marriage, yet we do not live with sadness. The reasons for this are:

We trust that children are blessings from the Lord and that He will give them to us in His time. He is the One who closes the womb and opens the womb. We are content with what God has given. Further, we have heard many testimonies where God blessed the couples with children after many years of marriage. So we do not lose hope. We also have a desire to adopt after some years. When we have a good understanding of the doctrine of God and His providence, we live with contentment, not sadness.

How have "complicating factors" shaped your marriage?

Cross-cultural marriage does have its own cultural package. However, if the focus is on being biblical, the couple and the family can come to neutral ground. From the beginning, we have decided to be more biblical in everything we do. That principle has been helping us to adjust from time to time by having a neutral aspect.

We are positive about adoption and learning about it theologically.

What has your marriage been able to do because it is happy? What has been the fruit of your marriage outside of your happiness?

As we have grown together as a Christian couple, it has been a strong witness in both the community we live in and the church. We have tried to set an example in our community of prioritizing marriage and family life. We practice hospitality toward unbelievers and believers, particularly those who are singles in the church.

What way would you like your marriage to be different in ten years?

To have children or adopt, facing the challenges of parenting and at the same time enjoying the blessings of children. To deal well with the challenges of Shiva's change of ministry.

What encouragement would you give to someone in an unhappy marriage?

First, the biblical understanding of marriage is important. Second, learn the differences in each other and biblically learn to overcome sin and help one another. Third, fulfill your own calling toward each other in the light of God's Word. Fourth, seek help from a godly couple and learn from their example. Fifth, the local church is vital in a happy marriage.

What is your favorite thing about being married?

Not being alone.
Having a companion and helpmeet.
Experiencing blessings as a couple, together.
Sharing each other's burdens and sorrows.
Having our own family for God's glory.

2

Oneness

This at last is bone of my bones
and flesh of my flesh;
she shall be called Woman,
because she was taken out of Man.
—Genesis 2:23

These are, of course, Adam's words upon seeing Eve. "At last"—a creature like him. Not bird, reptile, fish, insect, or mammal but another human made in God's image. Made of the same stuff. Made for the same purpose of glorifying God. Made for each other. This realization brought new joy, even in unfallen Eden. In the garden, there was nothing to interrupt the unity that Adam and Eve enjoyed, nothing to mar the perfect friendship that they had. It was oneness in every way, until sin established a divide. Since then, oneness has not been an effortless presence in marriage.

We often think of oneness in terms of physical union: "They shall become one flesh" (Gen. 2:24). This is true, but it is simply a single aspect of oneness. Because there is so much more to oneness than sex, there is more to achieving it than bed. Physical oneness is only one part of a healthy reality. Martin Bucer called a married couple's physical desire for each other "God's holy accomplishment of marital love."[1] It is a physical expression of a fuller love for each other: one way that spouses can communicate their devotion to each other and their joy in being united. Sexual union must be there, and even after the fall, it is still designed to bring happiness: "A man shall leave his father and his mother and hold fast to his wife, and they shall become one flesh" (Gen. 2:24; see also Matt. 19:5; Eph. 5:31).

But Paul also notes in 1 Corinthians 6:16–17 that a man becomes one flesh with a prostitute. If physical oneness can come through a one-night stand, then clearly, something deeper must be going on to create oneness in a healthy marriage. Commenting on a counseling case, Jordan Peterson states, "Maybe the physical intimacy they undoubtedly shared should have been matched, as it often is not, by a corresponding psychological intimacy."[2] "One flesh" has a fuller meaning than physical union alone. Physical union comes immediately in a marriage relationship, a forerunner and picture of the whole-person union that develops over the course of a marriage. This is one reason that spouses should find each other increasingly attractive—not less—even with physical age, because oneness has increased and, with it, the desire for intimacy in every way. The physical union is not unimportant—not at all! But it is not primary, which is why a marriage in which physical union is impossible because of illness, age, or disability can still have deep oneness. The "one flesh" relationship is one happy facet of the great gift of union.

Because union in a marriage facilitates joy, a lack of it saps happiness. Different opinions introduce friction. Different habits insert space. Different goals splinter a solid purpose. Different beds physically manifest an inner reality. Different gods establish divergent trajectories. Significant unresolved differences can lead to chronic strife, even violence, and a permanent fracture. Oneness is often something that we have to fight for, as circumstances and self continually pull spouses apart.

But there does not have to be stark division in order for there to be a lack of oneness. Do you remember Mr. and Mrs. Hurst from *Pride and Prejudice*? She is Mr. Bingley's sister and spends most of her time playing cards, the piano, and social games. He spends most of his time drinking and sleeping. Their peaceful marriage is striking: there is no conflict, no hostility. They have a very modern marriage—both partners living their own lives. But it is not the peace in their marriage that strikes you as you read the novel. It is the lack of oneness. And the lack of oneness lends the marriage a deadened quality. Both spouses are alive and well—even content at one level—but the relationship is a ghost of what it should be. All they have is what Robert Frost called "the slow, smokeless burning of decay": any benefit, any warmth weak and accidental, coming through the natural process of rot.[3] There is no friendship that brings life and binds them together.

A marriage can be like this if, like the Hursts, husband and wife carry on with their own interests and pursuits without bothering the other. When there is enough money or space or time, a couple can go through life with very little intervention or inconvenience from the other. But we all know that this is not a healthy marriage. Even Portia asked Brutus: "Am I your self / But, as it were, in sort or limitation, / To keep with you at meals, comfort your bed, / And talk to you sometimes / Dwell I but in the suburbs / Of your good pleasure?"[4] Peace and occasional intersection do not equal unity. Marriage is supposed to be union. It is designed to be oneness.

And oneness does not mean sameness. That is dull and effortless. Oneness is deep, loving knowledge of another person, and accommodating your life and likes to his or hers in the most intimate friendship. This cannot be occasional or casual. Real unity needs to be the substance of a relationship if that relationship is to bring joy. "Do two walk together, unless they have agreed to meet?" Amos asks (3:3).

But closeness can be tricky, can't it? In her novel *Agnes Grey*, Anne Brontë observes: "Habitual associations are known to exercise a great influence over each other's minds and manners. Those whose actions are ever before our eyes, whose words are ever in our ears, will naturally lead us, albeit against our will—slowly—gradually—imperceptibly, perhaps, to act and speak as they do."[5] Closeness to another sinner means that sin can and does rub off on each other. And it is easier to be dragged down than to pull someone up. In his poem "Locksley Hall," Tennyson has the speaker address a young bride: "Thou shalt lower to his level day by day, / What is fine within thee growing coarse to sympathize with clay. / As the husband, so the wife is: thou art mated with a clown, / And the grossness of his nature will have weight to drag thee down."[6] Closeness rarely tends to average out but leans to the lowest common denominator.

We see this right from the garden: it is Eve's very closeness to Adam that draws him into eating the fruit with her. When God confronts him with his own sin, Adam passes the blame on to Eve, "the woman whom you gave to be with me" (Gen. 3:12), whom he had called "bone of my bones and flesh of my flesh" just a few verses before (2:23). Following Adam's example, Eve blames another creature. Martin Luther points out that this issue probably came up throughout their multicentury marriage: "Eve would say, 'You ate the apple,' and Adam would retort, 'You gave it to me.'"[7] Closeness between sinners can be a very messy thing. Sometimes the influence is gradual enough to make it hard to see. Sometimes it is so obvious that the pain is immediate, as an issue such as debt, pornography, or violence relentlessly widens the gap. Sin does not bring real unity. It may seem to unify in the short term, but in the long run, evil is always divided against itself and spawns division.

Oneness can also be threatened by fear of vulnerability. This may be a legitimate fear in a bad marriage, but it is present to some degree in almost all marriages. Who likes being vulnerable? Vulnerability is disclosing very tender parts of ourselves to another person before we know exactly how he or she will respond. We do this in order to be known, deepen trust, and test love. We do it to gain oneness. But for fallen human beings, this is risky. By definition, vulnerability means potential hurt, and none of us want that. But we are called to it because vulnerability is connected to love. It is true in a marriage: the more you know your spouse, the more your spouse knows you, the more the potential for loving unity *and* for hurt increases. This is one reason that divorces are so painful: people have made themselves vulnerable in order to move toward oneness, and the oneness has been fractured, damaging the person who has exposed himself or herself. Invulnerability can look attractive. But God does not call us to invulnerability. He calls us to love—to oneness. C.S. Lewis said:

> To love at all is to be vulnerable. Love anything and your heart will be wrung and possibly broken. If you want to make sure of keeping it intact you must give it to no one, not even an animal.

> Wrap it carefully round with hobbies and little luxuries. . . . Lock it up safe in the casket . . . of your selfishness. But in that casket, safe, dark, motionless, airless, it will change. It will not be broken; it will become unbreakable.[8]

That is a frightening prospect, isn't it? In a marriage, the opposite of oneness is not independence but isolation. Perhaps not physical isolation, but emotional, psychological, and relational aloneness will be inevitable where unity is absent. Oneness comes from a willing giving of self to another out of love. It comes from the opposite of selfishness. Selfishness is the biggest threat to the oneness of a union because selfishness is the opposite of fellowship. It is orienting life around my wants and desires instead of loving my neighbor as I love myself and doing for that person what I would have him or her do for me. So facilitating fellowship is a major part in cultivating oneness.

This is usually something that we have to practice. Like sanctification, oneness in marriage is a work, not an act. Sometimes it starts with basic adjustments. Luther wrote: "There is a lot to get used to in the first year of marriage. One wakes up in the morning and finds a pair of pigtails on the pillow which were not there before."[9] Most things, though, take more adjustment than pigtails. Almost a hundred years ago, Dorothy Canfield wrote:

> Anybody who knows anything knows how delicate and exacting a matter it is to try to tune in harmony two human beings, almost constitutionally out of tune even with themselves, full of strange complicated weaknesses and unexpected beauties and strength. . . . Any fool can see that no outside complications are needed to make the problem a difficult one.[10]

All you have to do to create distance in a marriage is nothing.

Circumstances can make this harder. Distractions, even from good things such as career, leisure, hobbies, and children's schedules, can widen existing division. They consume time and energy that rightly belongs to the spouse. They divide our relational attention from where it should rightly be.

None of this sounds very happy, does it? Where is the blessing in oneness if it is rare, is almost unnatural, and requires the pain of vulnerability? Our culture is so awash in individualism that oneness can be hard to see, let alone rightly value. "They have never caught sight of this unity," said Martyn Lloyd-Jones; "they still think in terms of individuality, and so you have two people asserting their rights, and therefore you get clashes and discord and separation."[11] We need to understand that concept if we are to pursue unity. Because oneness in a marriage is designed to bring great joy to a couple, the marriage "has precedence over every other human relationship."[12]

Hudson Taylor, the nineteenth-century missionary to China, married a fellow missionary despite protests that he was her social inferior and things would never work for them as a couple. But the marriage turned out to be an amazingly fruitful as well as happy one. The oneness that Hudson and Maria shared made their union a powerhouse of gospel proclamation. One biographer wrote that "the overriding factor in their marriage was an equal, uninhibited loyalty to their vocation."[13] Hudson and Maria's unity came from a unified worldview and an orientation to life that revolved around the gospel. Every Christian marriage can experience the unity that is one side effect of glorifying and enjoying God.

Just as division is the fruit of sin, so unity is the fruit of the Spirit. We can, like the world, chase closeness as the means to our happiness, instead of realizing that both closeness and happiness are the joyful fruit of sanctification and fellowship with God. The blessedness of growing in the fruit of the Spirit—of becoming increasingly Christ-like—will necessarily bring the joy of oneness in a marriage.

Have you thought about the fruit of the Spirit in this way? As we grow in our own ability to love, we also become more lovable: a happy opposite of a vicious cycle. As the joy of our salvation deepens, we are more pleasant to be with. When the peace of God rules in our hearts, we are able to bring calm to those around us, as strife and discontentment die. A spouse growing in patience is easier and easier to live with. Real kindness that has the other's good at heart will be a blessing. Goodness builds trust and attracts people, especially a spouse! Faithfulness—an attribute that we often associate with marriage—brings security to a relationship existing in a faithless world. And developing self-control, in either restraining or exerting ourselves in different areas in accordance with Scripture, gives the stability of predictability and dependability.

Who would not want unity with someone characterized by these things? This is the kind of person who is a joy to be with as he or she brings comfort, encouragement, and groundedness to others. While growth in the fruit of the Spirit brings the primary blessing of increasing closeness with the Lord, it will inevitably increase unity in a Christian marriage.

If you live with someone who is marked by the fruit of the Spirit, you can tell that a challenge or penetrating question that the person asks is meant for your good, or that disagreement on an issue is fueled not by self-interest but by biblical conviction. If you are someone who is marked by the fruit of the Spirit, it will be easier to think the best of your spouse's words, actions, and motives, giving your spouse the benefit of the doubt. There will be not only an ability to work through differences in a way that honors the Lord, but a desire to do things in a way that reflects an awareness of living before God's face.

God designed sanctification to get rid of relational impediments. This is primarily true of our relationship with Him, as He makes us fit temples for the Spirit, preparing us to dwell with Him eternally. Sin has to be removed for this closeness to happen. But this is also true of our marriage relationships: increased holiness brings increased oneness. Growth in grace gets rid of the things that come between and damage fallen people in a fallen world. This progression in sanctification brings closeness to a marriage—the ability to become increasingly near each other in a way that brings more blessing than hurt.

When a husband and wife struggle with unity, they are more vulnerable to the discouragement of circumstances. Frustrations coming from work demands, the busyness of children, difficult relationships outside the home, and the frustration of aging bodies are all heavier when unity is lacking. There is a reason that unbelievers leave each other when facing major grief or health challenges.[14] Temptations also look more appealing when home is fractured: a lack of real unity is a massive opportunity for Satan to be at work on all sorts of fronts. A fractured marriage is not hard to batter from the outside, and this often leads to unfaithfulness.

The husband who is harsh or unloving, not living with his wife in understanding, and the wife who is a constant dripping on a rainy day, nagging and complaining, both leak unhappiness into the relationship, making it an unpleasant place to live. The guilt—oppressive or subconscious—of a distorted sex life drains happiness and the joy that God designed to go with the one-flesh union.

When we are aware of the blessing that oneness brings to a relationship, we will be on our guard against things that damage it. Part of the happiness that this unity brings is the ability to withstand external attacks. The adventure of a marriage faces all sorts of challenges as it progresses through time. A couple who are on the same page about intentionally living before the face of God will be difficult to distract from that all-important goal. Fixing our eyes on Jesus together enables us to run well together, synchronized not only in our drive and end destination, but also in how we get there. When spouses are aware of the world and the devil, and seek multifaceted refuge from them in Christ, the marriage is protected from attacks and temptations that would otherwise distract and even derail the relationship.

Commenting on the fellowship that God created in marriage, John Milton observed that it was made for "when we need / Refreshment, whether food, or talk between, / Food of the mind, or this sweet intercourse / Of looks and smiles, for smiles from Reason flow . . . and are of love the food."[15] Biblical oneness that produces the friendship of marriage nourishes a couple. Bucer explains such a friendship: "It means that out of love for his wife a husband chooses her above all other women and is so deeply attached to her that people will regard them as only one person."[16] The friendship of another Christian with whom you can be intimate in every way is designed to bring joy and, next to friendship with God, brings the deepest happiness that life holds.

Story (2010)

Sijin and Mina are from Seoul, where they met at church during their college years: Sijin was the leader of the small group that Mina joined. They were married in 2010 and are currently living abroad for Sijin's graduate studies. Mina does some formal counseling, and they have four children.

Do you have a happy marriage?

After we got married, we came to the United States for seminary training. Our first year was bitter and sweet. It was a challenging year with new environments and challenges as a couple. After that, we sure have had many ups and downs but can say that we've had a happy marriage with God's help and grace.

We've learned to be happy even in unhappy situations. For example, in the first few years of his life, our son had to undergo about fifteen surgeries under general anesthesia, including major procedures. While we were waiting for him in the hospital waiting room, nurses always encouraged us not to skip meals, so that we would be full of energy and ready to take care of him after the procedures. We usually went there without the older kids when we headed down to the hospital. When our son was younger, his health condition was much more fragile than it is now; we were afraid to leave him with a babysitter or even with our friend. Something major came up every six months for three years. And six weeks prior to any procedures, he couldn't get sick; otherwise, procedures must be rescheduled. So we did not think of having a date night as a couple. But whenever we went to the hospital, we were just the two of us, holding hands together and having Subway sandwiches together on the first floor of the children's hospital. At that time, we were grateful and found that our Subway sandwiches could be much better than nice and luxurious restaurant food. Of course, we could not enjoy our sandwiches as much as we wanted because of our son, but we still consider that time as our date. I [Sijin] knew that Mina was very anxious, and she knew that I was scared and worried, thinking of the outcome of the procedures. But over the sandwiches, we shared our tears and smiles, prayed together, encouraged each other, and recalled good memories. So I can say that I am happy, and I can be happy in difficult situations because my wife is with me.

How do you know that you have a happy marriage?

Because we hardly fight? I [Mina] would say, thanks to God and His grace, we've continued on our journey of sanctification. We continue to learn to love and forgive each other as our closest neighbors. We are praying together, making no secrets (having transparency), having lots of conversations, not being afraid of saying "sorry," and trying to think of each other first. We understand each other and each other's needs better than before. Despite our different personalities and preferences, we've shared more common things—values, ideas, and opinions in our life.

Has your marriage always been happy?

Sijin: I think that being happy means not just an emotional or feeling matter. A happy marriage is based on the trustworthy relationship between husband and wife. How can I say I have a happy marriage in unhappy situations (financial-wise, healthwise, etc.)?

Mina: I cannot say that it has always been happy. We've had good days and bad days—but more good days, I can say. And as I wrote above, our first year of marriage was rough.

I told my friends that marriage is not their answer if they pursue happiness in their lives. Marriage may bring happiness to some extent, but not the ultimate happiness. Sometimes (honestly, many times), married life is not easy; instead, it is more challenging. It's more about giving and serving rather than receiving and demanding, sacrificing rather than enjoying myself (my time, my hobbies, my friends), making commitments, and being more patient, loving, and forgiving. Married life is where we need to practice holiness and Christ's humility (Phil. 2).

I remember Tim Keller saying that "romance, sex, laughter, and plain fun are the by-products of [this] process of sanctification, refinement, glorification."[17] So is happiness, I think.

What things have you found that detract from happiness in your marriage?

Sijin: Seeking my own happiness, more than our happiness, in our marriage is a major detraction, like selfish thoughts, acts, and behaviors.

Mina: Looking to only my interests, untamed tongue (when I am angry), discontented heart, misunderstanding, comparing ourselves and our situations to others.

Also, as a couple living in a foreign country, we sometimes struggled with external factors—finding ways to maintain our visa status, having limited finances, not being eligible to work, planning our future, etc.

We know that those external factors should not hinder our marriage. Living in a foreign country can be a great opportunity to grow our faith and relationship as husband and wife. But we still recognize the reality of life, just like the Israelites were supposed to rely on their God in the wilderness and be bound together. However, their wilderness life was also challenging as they faced many life issues.

What are some things that your marriage has overcome to be at the place that it is now?

Ways of communication. Also, we have different channels to send and receive the message of love (a.k.a. love languages). We had to learn it hard and are still learning.

How do you deal with remaining sin in yourselves in marriage?

Sijin: We talk a lot together. We have been sharing everything we are thinking, doing, and wanting. But we understand and agree that we should come individually to talk to God as our priority.

Mina: We gently rebuke each other's sins if needed. And we bring each other's attention to one another when we find each other's shortcomings/flaws, which should be corrected.

I've found that sin is very contagious and influential on each other (and even in the family). Likewise, showing grace and love to one another is contagious. If he blamed me, I tried to find things to blame him for. If he complained, I complained. If he said "sorry," I said "sorry." If he yields one thing, I can yield two things.

I recently read one article titled "Mirrors Work Best from the Front" as I prepared a counseling session. It summarized well that I need to examine myself in the light of God's Word first before pointing my finger at my husband and his sin. I am trying to be diligent in my prayers and reading God's Word and finding my own logs in my eye (Matt. 7).

What things have you noticed that drain happiness?

Sijin: When we follow the criteria of happiness that the secular world seeks. There are not many things I can bring to my spouse, from secular standpoints. But I do not mean that we have to be separated from the world.

Mina: I want to focus on my heart issue. Because the heart is the spring of life (Prov. 4:23; Mark 7), everything I think, speak, and do flows from my heart. When I have a hardened and thorny heart or whenever something troubles my heart, I am neither patient, loving, caring, nor listening. I find myself judging, blaming, and complaining.

Are there any habits or patterns that establish or perpetuate happiness?

Sijin: Practically speaking, I try to remember that I'm a weak vessel, and that Mina is a weaker vessel (1 Peter 3:7).

Mina: Checking in with him on how he is doing during the day. Asking him how I could pray for him today or this week.

Who are your marriage role models? Why?

Sijin: Besides our perfect example of Jesus, who loves His bride that is the church, I sometimes think John and Olive. They were the oldest members of my home church. Personally, I didn't have chances to get to know them very well. I saw them every Lord's Day, entering the sanctuary and holding their hands together. And I hear that they never argued with each other. That left me a big question: "How?"

Mina: Sijin and I both came from broken families. We still respect and love our parents, but we didn't capture what biblical marriage looks like from our experiences as we grew up. I had cynical attitudes toward marriage. After we came to the States and the church circle, we met godly couples, and we want to follow their examples. Four older couples who were professors and their spouses were especially formative. I can add more, but these four couples are special to me as I've known them and their marriage life directly and indirectly. In common, I see their love for Christ and His church and people and their mature love for their spouses and families. They are respectful and faithful to each other and grateful for each other.

Can you share one story or event that shaped or shifted your relationship, or made you think differently about your spouse?

Sijin: I lost my mind from time to time when my youngest son was in the hospital due to his heart defects. I was happy and grateful to share Mina and my darkest moments together.

Mina: The past five years with our youngest son. Sijin has shared everything with me, many thoughts, many smiles, and many tears.

He shows his care and love for me and the kids and leads us to draw close to God whenever we have difficult days.

Also, I can add that he always initiated reconciliation first during our first year of marriage. He was not afraid of saying "sorry" first, while I was very stubborn.

How do you live with the sadness of a fallen world in a good marriage?

Our son's condition is still sad and still hard, but we have a good God. With His grace and help, we are here counting the blessings the Lord has given to us and our family. With our son's health journey (along with other medical/health issues the other kids have), God has brought us together as husband and wife, as a team, rejoicing and crying together, walking together, praying together, holding hands together. When I [Mina] was depressed and weak, Sijin pointed me to Christ by sending Scriptures and Psalms. And I prayed with and for him when he went down to the pit emotionally. Through sadness, God has shaped our bond to be more robust.

When we sat with a pastor when I was pregnant, he encouraged us and prayed with and for us. And we still hold very dear to our hearts what he shared with us: we could deserve worse things. But God is gracious. This truth is still alive in our lives, day by day. God has been merciful to us.

Also, we have the greatest hope in Jesus Christ that He will wipe all our tears and show us His glory one day. There will be no sorrow and pain. And our son will have a perfect heart. "And after you have suffered a little while, the God of all grace, who has called you to his eternal glory in Christ, will himself restore, confirm, strengthen, and establish you" (1 Peter 5:10).

What has your marriage been able to do because it is happy? What has been the fruit of your marriage outside of your happiness?

To break through some hardships together. To live another day together. To continue this journey together.

Thinking of the fruit, we think of the fruit of the Spirit. We can both say that we have been growing in love, joy, peace, patience, kindness, goodness, faithfulness, gentleness, and self-control through our marriage.

What encouragement would you give to someone in an unhappy marriage?

This is one of my [Mina's] favorite Jay Adams quotes: "The Christian home, then, is a place where sinful persons face the problems of a sinful world. Yet they face them together with God and His resources, which are all centered in Christ. Sinners live in the Christian home, but the sinless Savior lives there too. That is what makes the difference!"[18]

Also, you probably know the "marriage triangle": the closer that a husband and wife draw to Christ, the closer they draw to each other.

What is your favorite thing about being married?

Experiencing/tasting the mystery Paul talks about in Ephesians 5:25–33, which also refers to Christ and His church! Having companionship and friendship. Enjoying the blessings God has given to us, including our children.

3

Personhood

So God created man in his own image,
in the image of God he created him;
male and female he created them.
—Genesis 1:27

One of the incredible things about creation is its diversity. If you look at a drop of pond water under a good microscope, you will see an astounding range of living things on the slide. Multiple plants and animals (strange ones!) float in the water, often with bits of minerals. God's creation is full of surprising variety. Such diversity extends to human creation. Each person is made in God's image, each fallen and finite, each body and soul destined for eternity, each valuable, but each different. The wonder of personhood is dim to us only because it is ubiquitous. It is everywhere we look and we are part of it, so it can be hard to see. We climb mountains or visit remote coastlines to marvel at creation, when the driver's license office may be even more spectacular—if we only had eyes for the wonder of created personhood.

God did not make people clones. While humans are one "kind," the variety within humanity is staggering, and evidence of how particular God is in His creation. Between nature and nurture—we might call that small-scale creation and providence—God fashions each particular human. The image of God in every person expresses aspects of the Lord who made us and takes care of us. Some shared attributes, such as anger, are often twisted through the fall, but the capacities for creativity, innovation, love, thought, and dominion all find varied expression in the human creation that was the crown to the six days of God's creative work. Each man, woman, and child has unique being and purpose and thought.

This has implications for marriage and is part of God's design for the relationship. A recognition of our spouses' personhood really is a lived-out acknowledgment of their fundamental identity. As part of God's creation, our spouses have individuality: unique status as human beings made in God's image. This extends far beyond their created bodies. God also made their minds, hearts, and souls. Each person is a different mix of genetics and family culture, history, and experience, which make the person who he or she is. The person has his or her own gifts and abilities, likes and loathings, interests, strengths, and failings. Personality is a large part of this, but personhood goes even deeper. Before this person is your spouse—and long after he or she is your spouse—the person is his or her own self before God, totally apart from you.

This concept might not sound like the fast track to oneness, but Scripture teaches both things: unity in marriage and a sanctified individualism. We have looked at oneness already. Unity is fundamental in a marriage. It is a source of great joy. The idea of personhood in Scripture is repeatedly shown in the importance of everyone's individual choices in Psalm 1; the consequences of our actions in Matthew 25, Luke 12, and Romans 2; and the primacy of our relationship to God, both as a creature and as a redeemed sinner. Even after the best, holiest marriage, each person will stand on his or her own before God to give an account and receive a reward for deeds done in the flesh. A biblical marriage promotes unity *and* values personhood, as Scripture itself does.

In some passages, such as 1 Corinthians 7, the two concepts of unity and personhood overlap: "The husband should give to his wife her conjugal rights, and likewise the wife to her husband" (v. 3). Here, even corporeal individuality in decided giving creates oneness. Unity and individuality become tangled in a way that can make it difficult to discern where one starts and ends, but they are both there.

So biblical individualism is not autonomy. In other words, it is not my calling the shots, defining myself, and pursuing independence. Instead, it is a recognition that we are each created by God for a particular purpose, and each in need of His saving grace and the holiness without which no one will see the Lord. Biblical individualism involves accountability and distinct roles, value, and limitations. This is why it is compatible with and complementary to oneness.

Since the Bible teaches both unity and individuality, they will not be contradictory in a Christian marriage. Instead, the idea of personhood brings blessing. It gives our marriages interest, allowing us to enjoy variety. It gives us freedom, releasing us from burdens that we are not designed to bear. And it also gives us responsibility, understanding Scripture's requirements of us in relation to personhood.

The idea of personhood in marriage gives us the happiness of enjoying our spouses' gifts as deliberate blessings from God in their unique callings. Because our spouses are each their own person, we can be interested in their strengths and talents not just as they relate to us as our spouses, but also as who they are as individuals, serving the Lord in church and community. So often, these are the things that attract us to someone before marriage: conversational skills, a healthy work ethic, creative involvement with friends and family, athletic ability, or musical talent. After marriage, we can enjoy these even more. We can see service and gifts and talent and particular sacrifice better than anyone else, and so we can be more thankful for it and encouraged by it. We can more deeply enjoy the display of gifts in this person with whom we share life. We can be drawn into the person's interests—our own horizons broadened by another set of utilized strengths and gifts.

And being interested fosters being interesting: there is a healthy feedback loop here. As we enjoy our spouses' use of their unique gifts, they feel and value it and are encouraged in using them. Someone who tries to use his or her gifts in an atmosphere of inferiority or invisibility will soon lose zeal: practicing a skill or exercising a gift in an environment of criticism or dismissal makes further effort feel pointless. But the opposite is also true. Even common skills that we use daily—in work, parenting, or recreation—become sweeter when they are met with recognition and appreciation. Encouragement blesses even the most independent people, and unity becomes a fruit of recognizing individuality.

Being conscious of personhood also gives us the freedom of getting to know this other human being on a level that nobody else does. Another person, indwelled by the Holy Spirit, is something that we will never come to the bottom of in this life. We do not fully understand ourselves, let alone someone else, so in marriage we can enjoy the privilege of a lifetime of study and discovery. Do you remember the scene in *Pride and Prejudice* at Netherfield in which Mr. Darcy calls country society "confined and unvarying"? Lizzy fires back, "But people themselves alter so much, that there is something new to be observed in them forever."[1] She is right. It is true even in the constant closeness of a marriage; there is always something new. Despite established life patterns and personalities, people are always changing. So there are always new things to observe. Sanctification is an incredibly interesting process! And it is a joy to watch, even if it comes, as it so often does, through pain. If you are in a Christian marriage, then you have a front-row seat for watching God make another believer increasingly Christlike. Things are always changing, and it is an exclusive honor to see this up close.

Knowing that your spouse is his or her own person will also give you the freedom to respect the unique likes, dislikes, and interests that your spouse has. Daily disunities in the little things have the potential to create friction and resulting heat. Maybe it is a preference in how the laundry is folded or the grass is cut or what is for supper, but respecting your spouse's personhood can smooth things out here. Our spouses were made in God's image, not ours, and they have their own preferences!

We live in a time when cheerful, adaptable, mildly extroverted personalities are the cultural gold standard. They are the easiest to live with! Even John Owen, writing centuries ago, noted this: "Some are naturally of a more tranquil and quiet temper than others. These people are comparatively peaceable and useful to others."[2] This perspective is especially true in the twenty-first-century West. People who do not fit this profile tend to be seen as aberrant. We have fewer eccentrics: people whose personalities make others uncomfortable by their intensity or introversion or grief. The characters who populated Dickens' novels do not live in middle-class America, at least not publicly. This does not mean that there is never a time for behavioral intervention. And though certain personalities are prone to certain sins, we can never blame a personality for sin any more than we can blame circumstances for sin. Personality itself is part of divine creation and divine creativity. Each personality, though fallen, has something unique to offer, some role to play that another cannot, some perspective to show that another is unable to see. In marriage, personality is a factor that affects daily life and gives it great interest. Respecting that gives both spouses freedom to enjoy activities and ideas and blessings that we might not naturally see or appreciate. There is happiness in appreciating our spouses for being themselves.

Winston Churchill was not an easy man. The story goes that one female MP actually told him, "If you were my husband, I'd put poison in your coffee!" (He retorted that if *she* were his wife, he would drink it.) But a biographer wrote about Winston and his wife, Clementine: "Their completely different temperaments . . . found a clear appreciation of each other." "Their marriage never would have worked had it been otherwise."[3] We can value our spouses for who they are, not just what they do. It is easy, as the years flow on and husbands and wives follow the same routines, month after month, to blur our spouses with their role, to confuse who they are with their function in the relationship: the one who primarily cares for the children, or makes the bulk of the income, or schedules everyone's social lives. While associations can be inevitable, making a human synonymous with a function or limited role is degrading. An older couple in a congregation I was part of had been empty-nesters for decades but never used each other's names. Instead, it was "Mamma" and "Papa." Their marriage had revolved around their children, and though those children were long gone, with older children of their own, this couple was unable to separate each other from the roles that had been most important in their lives. They had lost part of each other's personhood and could not—or would not—regain it. That is a relational as well as a humanitarian failure. We get to value our spouses as God's creation, not as a relational function.

But then we can value what they do because *they* did it, and that makes it more valuable to us than mere functionality. The order matters—personhood, then role—and there is great freedom in this logic, a freedom that brings closeness as we recognize, appreciate, and enjoy. When spouses continue working day after day to faithfully fulfill their calling out of love to God but also care for the family, love makes that work more valuable to us. They are doing it because they care, not simply because they have to. There is certainly blessing in that.

And this idea of individuality also gives us the responsibility to challenge our spouses in places where they need that. Because marriage is not an end in itself, and because we will each stand alone before God at the end, we have the freedom to challenge and question wrong things, even if this temporarily disrupts the peace in our marriages. The pattern set out in Matthew 18 is not only for church relationships, but for marriages, too.

Perhaps this is especially important for women to remember. Very often, believers who rightly value the Bible can push past what is written, falling into reaction against cultural norms. A very unbiblical, imbalanced headship can be the ugly fruit. As Christian wives, we are to respect our husbands—not be in awe of them. Part of respecting them as people means that we respect the reality that they live before God's face, and they need to be respectfully confronted if they start to forget that. Sanctification and the fight against sin do not neutralize a personality: they use the strengths and root out the weak parts. They maximize this aspect of creation for God's glory. Our job is not to conform our spouses to ourselves or to some extrabiblical ideal that we have for them but to facilitate their conforming to Christ as whole persons, body, mind, and soul. Kindly and humbly calling out our spouses' sin helps them put to death the old man—actually helping them become more human, more fully who they were created to be and who they really are in Christ.

It also helps us to become more balanced. We are all prone to little quirks and obsessions that distort us, in all sorts of facets of our personhood. The Lord told us that it is not good for man to be alone—and that was in unfallen Eden! In our sinful state, our personalities need the balance of a spouse to help keep them in proportion. A good understanding of personality combined with loving truth can keep us from becoming caricatures of ourselves and help us stay proportional in ways that are spiritually, emotionally, intellectually, and socially healthy.

At the same time, a sanctified individualism also takes away the burden of feeling that we are ultimately responsible for our spouses. Now, we are certainly responsible for the way that we live with our spouses, the way that we treat them and help them grow in the fruit of the Spirit. But we are not all-sufficient. We are creatures, too, and do not bear ultimate responsibility for our spouses' safety, joy, satisfaction, sanctification, or evaluation. We cannot bear another human's fallen personhood. We cannot be everything that he or she needs. That burden is too great for one mere human being to bear for another, so it does not have to come between us or slow us down as we walk beside each other. Instead, Christ offers Himself as the infinite person who bears and redeems fallen personhood. We are not a savior; we have a Savior. Living in that reality gives great freedom in a marriage.

And this is connected to something deeper. A biblical view of personhood also means, despite the closeness that this reality fosters in a relationship, that some things are off-limits to us simply because we are another creature. We need to be careful here, because this cannot mean that there should not be free openness, honesty, and ability to ask questions, express concerns, confess sin, and share our deepest dreams, disappointments, frustrations, and joys. There should be that; there must be that—it is all essential in a marriage, and it needs to happen. Unity should be deep and extensive. Friendship must be genuine and trusted. But our spouses, like us, are fully known only to God. We may know them better than any other human does, but even after a lifetime, it will not come close to God's knowledge of them. And that is the relationship that has primacy, because that relationship is the source and chief end of personhood. That is the relationship that cannot be violated or usurped, especially by a godly marriage.

Our culture holds up the idea of a soulmate: that one person who knows everything about you and whom you tell everything. We have imbibed so much of this concept that we often cannot see that it is not only impossible but also not right, simply because the spousal relationship should not be the ultimate one. The idea that spouses do not and should not have 100 percent access to each other shocked me the first time that I heard it verbalized, but I have heard it from several elderly, godly people with long and happy marriages and seen it in many more. This idea can be twisted, used as an excuse to conceal or withdraw, but that will not bring trust or joy. And this acknowledgment of these relational limits makes biblical sense. As much as we are to study each other and know each other and share each other, there are places that we are not able to go, simply because we are another creature. We are not absolute. Personhood was made for intimacy, not omniscience.

In T.S. Eliot's poem "The Wasteland," he describes a couple who are sitting at home in the evening, and the wife keeps nattering on: "Speak to me. . . . Speak. / What are you thinking of? What thinking? What? / I never know what you are thinking. Think."[4] She erodes the relationship by her constant grasping at her husband's mind and heart. If we were called to be the ultimate sanctifiers and managers of our spouses, we would need omniscience. Since we are not, we do not need it. We would not be able to bear such a burden. Instead, we can release our spouses to the Lord by acknowledging this primary relationship. We do it not in blind faith but out of love for our spouses and trust in our Creator. In a healthy marriage, a respect for personhood and the Lord's absolute right in each other's lives means that you both have the freedom to go to the other out of a need for fellowship and companionship—a willingness to share and be shared—not because you have a need to control what is going on in the other person's heart and head. This goes back to the idea that before this person is your spouse—and long after he or she is your spouse—the person is his or her own self before God, totally apart from you. Respecting the primacy of this relationship is part of respecting our spouses' personhood and seeing how we can help them grow in it.

Personhood itself is a gift. In this fractured and changing world, our personhood means that our link with our Creator is unbreakable and permanent. It gives us an anchor. In marriage, that anchor of personhood gives stability and healthy limitations. It adds depth and color to the blessing of union. And it respects not only the Lord's creativity in crafting each of us but also the bounds that He has included in that creation and the happiness for which He designed them.

Story (2009)

Theo and Carol met on eHarmony in the fall of 2007, met in person the following January, and have been married since 2009. Carol is a medical doctor; after years of engineering, Theo is now in pastoral ministry. They live in a small Canadian town.

Do you have a happy marriage?

Yes.

Carol: I am always happy to see Theo at the end of the day, and I find joy and fulfillment in being Theo's wife.

Theo: I look forward to sharing every day with Carol.

What makes your marriage happy?

We seek to keep Christ at the center of our marriage. Also finding ways to deliberately and joyfully serve each other.

Has it always been happy?

Theo: I wouldn't say that it wasn't happy, but there were times when life was unhappy (unemployment, career changes, health crises), and that reality was reflected in our marriage.

Carol: I have never not wanted to continue our marriage, but there were definitely hard times when we were not walking in tune with each other or with the Lord. Early on in our marriage, we were both pretty self-centered and were coasting in our spiritual walk. Our priorities were very earthly, and because of that we couldn't find satisfaction in meeting those goals. The Lord stopped us by sending hard providences our way, leading to a few very hard years that forced us to reevaluate everything.

How did it get to where it is now?

Theo: The grace of the Lord, prayer, and a conscious dying to self for the other's good.

Carol: Much like Theo's answer. A specific prayer I had early on was for Theo to be the leader of our home. When that prayer began to be answered, I found myself needing to pray for humility and a changed spirit to follow Theo's lead.

What things have you found that detract from happiness in your marriage?

Theo: Busyness, not taking time to just be together.

Carol: Bulldozing ahead with my preferred plans without deliberately engaging in discussion and spending time in prayer together. Letting anxiety get too much hold on me.

How do you deal with remaining sin in yourselves in marriage?

Theo: Prayer, looking to the Lord to realign my priorities with His, humility to accept correction when I have done wrong or have wrong priorities.

Carol: That hour of personal devotions in the morning is absolutely essential, so refusing to compromise on it; also, being accountable to Theo and listening when he (gently) brings up areas I struggle in.

What things have you noticed that drain happiness?

Theo: Any compromise in family worship patterns, not getting my exercise in, cluttered house, trying to "staycation" at home.

Carol: Not being able to detach from work (on-call duties), prolonged in-law visits, lack of sleep, feeling unheard, and overcommitting.

How would a compromise in family worship patterns disrupt happiness?

That idea stems back to a stretch when we ate out a lot (I [Carol] was too distracted to cook decent meals), and we wouldn't consistently do family devotions after eating out. I was on call around the clock and struggled to put my phone away for mealtimes. So even if we were home, my phone would be beeping and ringing and causing distraction, so Theo would lose his train of thought and things would spiral. A big change we made was having a consistent home-cooked family supper with devotions and (try to) keep the phones out of the dining room. At the very least, phone ringers are turned off. We also make a point of doing devotions either before or after we head out if we do eat out.

Are there any habits or patterns that establish/perpetuate happiness?

Theo: Regular family vacations as well as vacation without the kids every so often (we aim for once every five years), making a point of putting down the books and phones and being together at the end of most days.

Carol: Picking up or making things that I know Theo enjoys (e.g., his favorite beverage, doughnuts, a good steak), making sure things get tidied up, regular intimacy, playful teasing.

Who are your marriage role models? Why?

Theo: Our pastor and his wife: seeing how they participate together in ministry and balance the context of both partners' working while still maintaining their appropriate roles and appearing to be very happily married. Although my parents are happily married, their dynamic is very, very different from our marriage.

Carol: My parents: they learned early on to rely on each other (they were immigrants with no other family members around) and find contentment within their marriage. They disagree with each other respectfully and work out solutions.

How have career changes shifted your relationship or made you think differently about your spouse?

Theo: I feel more keenly the responsibility of leading my household in such a way that I am qualified for ministry. I also did not want to burden my family unduly with the added financial burdens of going back to school, so tried to be very diligent in getting my studies done well without dragging them on forever. I make deliberate time in my schedule for us to be together as a family and see those moments as precious.

Carol: My role became more defined. I see my role as freeing Theo up for ministry. It was harder to want to free him up to climb the corporate ladder. Now my goal is very much to manage the schedules and household tasks to maximize the energy he can put into his ministry. I try to keep my job as a lower priority than our marriage, taking care of the children and furthering Theo's work.

You both work outside the home and have young children: can you talk a bit about how you balance this?

This continues to be an area of juggling. As in the previous question, I [Carol] see my role as freeing Theo up for ministry, so I do try to shoulder the household management (making childcare work, arranging a housecleaner, meal planning, laundry, etc.). I held back on having a family practice for several years while Charis needed me to be flexible. The downside to that was needing to be available by phone almost around the clock. Now that Charis and Connell are both in school, I have started a practice that keeps me busy during their school days but has minimal after-hours commitment. Being self-employed allows me to tailor my schedule to ensure I'm available to take Charis to her appointments or stay home on teacher in-service days, holidays, etc. I'm a wife, a mom, then a doctor.

Theo has wanted to make a deliberate effort to spend time with the kids after the three seminary years of perhaps less-than-optimal time with them. Their bus stop is at the church, so he puts them on the bus in the morning and takes them home at the end of the day and spends that forty-five-ish minutes before I get home with them.

We both have learned to be more flexible in our scheduling and have found it necessary to make sure family life is a priority to make it work. Some weeks, though, are really strained and tough to get through.

How do you live with sadness in a good marriage?

Theo: It took years to figure that out, and we're still working on that. In summary, grace, faith in Christ, and continued growth in Him. We've had to really learn how to communicate to each other and accept that sometimes our processing is different. We had a three-year stretch of being on edge and tense between our second son's death, our daughter's adoption, and the subsequent discovery of her various health issues. We learned and continue to learn to give each other grace while also trying to be careful not to slip into sinful ways of coping.

Carol: I initially struggled to share grief. We had five miscarriages, and one of our sons died in infancy. Theo was always there to hold me while I cried. The day that our son was sent to NICU, Theo turned to me and said, "Here is where the rubber hits the road: either we trust God to carry us through and start praying and talking about these things, or we're done." He showed leadership and pointed me to Christ.

During our three really hard years, we learned to recognize that grief has common emotions but unique patterns and to not make assumptions about the other person based on their pattern of grief. Sometimes different is not bad or good—just different. We also needed to learn when to be vulnerable and seek out mature brothers and sisters in Christ to advise, comfort, and even reprove.

The trials we went through were excruciating, and we both made a lot of mistakes. God, however, used them for good. He pointed us to Himself and turned our lives back to Himself. Ultimately, He is the reason we are still together and happier in our marriage than before the trials.

How have "complicating factors" shaped your marriage?

We come from very different denominational backgrounds and cultural heritages. It has given us a richer experience of marriage by increasing our perspectives. It has also forced us to communicate and find common ground in our salvation.

Adoption forces extreme introspection and was exceedingly uncomfortable at times but again forced that communication between us. It also reminded us that nothing happens outside of God's providence. After a long stretch of hard providences, it was a reminder that God always gives good gifts to His children and He really does work all things for our good and His glory.

What has your marriage been able to do because it is happy?

Theo: By the grace of God, we have weathered storms that often split marriages apart. I have had personal health issues, suffered months of unemployment, struggled with depression in addition to our son's sickness and death, our daughter's adoption and health challenges. We've had our house flood and have moved multiple times. Because God blessed me with a happy marriage, it is worth fighting for when the waves come.

Carol: We never had to do any of those hard things alone. God carried us through extremely trying times and gave us each other to support each other through the bad times and to multiply our joy in the good times. We have had the opportunity to come alongside other grieving couples and show them that the Lord is good and kind, even in affliction.

What has been the fruit of your marriage outside of your happiness?

We have two loving, inquisitive, smart, and hilarious children here that we get to watch grow in stature and, we pray, in the fear of the Lord. We also have souls waiting for us in heaven.

What encouragement would you give to someone in an unhappy marriage?

Prayer is such a blessing. Pour out your sorrows and disappointments to the Lord and trust that He is working this for your good and His glory. Also, be sure to look at your patterns of interaction: Are you able to serve each other? Can you find joy in that service, knowing it is unto the Lord?

What is your favorite thing about being married?

Theo: Having someone to come home to at the end of every day; someone who understands me, loves me, and wants my good; someone who wishes to serve Christ and pushes me to serve Christ more fully.

Carol: Not needing to make all the decisions; being able to follow and hand over control.

4

Children

Did he not make them one, with a portion of the Spirit
in their union? And what was the one God seeking?
Godly offspring.
—Malachi 2:15

In a culture where career is paramount, environmentalism is a religion, and the economy is unpredictable, some couples openly choose childlessness. For other couples, children function as high-cost accessories through which parents display their taste, wealth, and connections. Many people see their children as conflicting with other goals and ideals, since they make us tired, fill our time, damage our bodies, and can be annoying and disappointing. Our culture has no issue with abortion as a preventive solution to these issues. In such a context, the church stands out in its view of children. Christian marriages—regardless of the presence of children in a particular marriage—should reflect the value of children. Believers can demonstrate that children really are a gift, part of God's design for marriage, part of the joy, instead of something that detracts from it.

Saying that God designed children to bring happiness to a marriage may sound strange if you or a Christian couple whom you love are struggling to have children. It may even sound unfeeling or cruel. But the grief of infertility—one impact that this broken world can have on a marriage—emphasizes God's design. The longing for children, and the emptiness of not having them, confirms that children are a gift from the Lord, as Scripture tells us. God designed us to multiply and find joy in that. The inability to do so can bring tension in a marriage: Rachel turns to Jacob, demanding, "Give me children, or I shall die!" Jacob responds in anger, "Am I in the place of God, who has withheld from you the fruit of the womb?" (Gen. 30:1–2). Even without tension like this, infertility often brings deep sadness to a marriage. But that very grief can be a testimony to the goodness of God's design. Sadness at the brokenness that infertility manifests can actually point to God's original plan for Christian marriage, even when a particular marriage keenly feels the sharpness of the fall.

But there are also couples who do have children, who have enjoyed the happiness of being daddy and mommy, who have poured their lives into a son or daughter, and whose lives have been emotionally upended by the grown child's rejection of their love. This deep grief, too, starkly shows how fallen things are. Instead of being supports and encouragements to parents, showing gratitude for all their teaching and care, some children reject God's pattern and call, turning their backs on their parents and their parents' God. Loving parents who faithfully endure rejection and even abuse by their own children know and show the evil of this sin.

Both these fracturings—the grief of a broken world and the grief of broken people—can be common to any marriage, Christian or not. The griefs of infertility and rejection by a child are often things that unbelievers experience and can also sympathize with. And these sadnesses both show the goodness of God's original design. The absence of loving parent-child relationships emphasizes the happiness that comes when God blesses a couple with children, and especially when He blesses those children with Himself.

Biblically, a husband and wife's sexual union is connected to procreation. Yet children are not the only reason—or even the primary reason—that God gave us sex. The Westminster Confession of Faith gives three biblical reasons for marriage, and children is not the first one: "Marriage was ordained for the mutual help of husband and wife [Gen. 2:18], for the increase of mankind with legitimate issue, and of the church with an holy seed [Mal. 2:15]; and for preventing of uncleanness [1 Cor. 7:2, 9]" (24.2). The marriage service in the Book of Common Prayer moved from a more Roman Catholic treatment of sex, which was essentially legitimized by children, to a biblical understanding that marriage is for "the hallowing of the union betwixt man and woman" before "the procreation of children."[1] Marriage is primarily designed for companionship. This is why a childless couple are not less married than a couple with children. Scripture shows this from the beginning: God creates Eve because it is not good for man to be alone; Adam needs a helpmeet. Then comes the command to multiply. The Song of Solomon is an ode to marital intimacy, and there is not a cradle or diaper in sight.

And although sex is certainly more than procreation, the two are clearly connected: as Christians, we recognize that children are a significant aspect of a couple's physical union. Our culture has used technology in entertainment and medicine to divide sex from procreation, linking it only with personal pleasure. We live in a cultural atmosphere that breathes out this message in a million ways. But the physical expression of love for each other in a marriage must never be conceptually severed from the idea of children and family. At the very least, a couple's sexual relationship ought to be deepening and strengthening their own relationship, making the home a stronger, happier place for children. It is not an accident that Jesus welcomes little children to Him immediately after teaching about marriage (Matt. 19:1–15). Whenever children come, however they come, a Christian marriage must always be a safe and welcoming place for children: planned or surprising, healthy or unwell, biological or adopted. This does not preclude wise and biblical use of family planning; it means that no matter how the Lord gives us children, they are to be welcomed.

Children, Scripture reminds us again and again, are a blessing. Some of the happiest parts of the Bible include the arrival of a baby. The blessing of children is remarkable. Psalm 127 is famous for its description: "Behold, children are a heritage from the LORD, the fruit of the womb a reward. . . . Blessed is the man who fills his quiver with them!" (vv. 3, 5).

In addition to clear statements such as these about the blessing of covenantal heritage, the Bible's narratives are often shaped by the joy of welcoming children, sometimes against a backdrop of the grief of infertility or rebellion. After losing their first sons—one to death, one to sin—Adam and Eve were comforted by Seth's birth (Gen. 4:25). Isaac's arrival was a monumental event, both for redemptive history and for his parents. There was joy for his parents that reverberates to this day: "God has made laughter for me; everyone who hears will laugh over me" (21:6). The accounts go beyond Genesis, with the arrivals of babies such as Obed, Samuel, and Solomon in the Old Testament, leading their parents to worship: "My heart exults in the LORD; my horn is exalted in the LORD" (1 Sam. 2:1).

The first birth in the New Testament—John the Baptist's—not only brought joy to his parents, who stood united in the face of interfering relatives (Luke 1:57–63), but also became the event that heralded Christ's birth (vv. 76–79). Mary's delivery of Jesus in that stable brought a happiness into the world that will grow through eternity. Interestingly, we can see the effect on His parents' relationship. Once Joseph understood Mary's God-given situation, the couple were united in their calling of this unique parenthood (Matt. 1:24–25). Scripture even records their shared concern when their young son was missing after a trip to Jerusalem: "Behold, your father and I have been searching for you in great distress" (Luke 2:48). The blessing of children is not only for the propagation of humanity but also for the development of a marriage and a couple's closeness.

God did not have to create conception, pregnancy, and childbirth. He spoke worlds into existence, and He certainly could have set up some sort of spontaneous generation for humans. He created myriads of angels to serve Him, but when He brought humanity into existence, He created two people: a man and woman who would become father and mother. In giving us conception and pregnancy, God allows us to participate in bringing other people into existence—we are allowed to be active in creating and developing another human. God uses us to bring a little human into the world who often bears our image as well as the Lord's (Gen. 5:3). Conception and pregnancy are a small picture of God's original creating: bringing life out of the dark void. There is wonder in that: the joy of sex producing the joy of new life.

It also produces a natural bond. This is one reason, John Chrysostom says, that God designed children to go with marriage: "For why do we not all spring up out of the earth? . . . In order that both the birth and bringing up of children, and the being born of another, might bind us mutually together."[2] The experience of having children not only gives a couple the privilege of participation in new creation, but also gives them bonds that grow through and out of that.

Labor and delivery itself can—and should—build a marriage. Despite being a consequence of the curse (Gen. 3:16), the very suffering involved can bind a couple together. What faithful husband can see his wife in pain and distress and not feel deeper love and care? Humans are wired to have sympathy when they see suffering; it is even more true in a close relationship and when the suffering is an act of love. Ask a new Christian father what the delivery room did to his view of his wife, suffering for a child she has not yet met, and the answer often involves something like this: "She is incredible" or "I respect her so much." From the wife's side, seeing a husband's care and receiving his support through delivery bring happiness even in pain. To know that someone is there, in your corner, willing to do anything—even if he can do nothing!—is a comfort.

And then the baby arrives. It is astounding that God entrusts a helpless creature with an eternal soul to sinful and inexperienced parents. And while it can feel overwhelming and deeply humbling, joy is certainly part of that. There is a purity to the marvel of a newborn. "Just think," an older woman said to me of a man who had destroyed himself through addictions, "when he was born, someone looked at his little fingers and was amazed." For a baby to come through development and birth, millions of unseen things need to go right, and when they do, there is happiness.

There is joy in watching a baby grow—the tiny toes and first smiles, the growth and development that happen at near-miraculous rates in those first years. Despite the sleep deprivation and need to learn many new skills, parents are privileged to have the blessing of children—the heritage that is God's reward far and above anything that we deserve.

But this rapid development and joy require intense work from the parents. Children enter the world helpless, unsanctified, and incredibly needy. The work of raising a child is initially physically demanding, with night feedings, carrying, buckling in, laundry, toilet training, and so much more. As children develop and grow more capable themselves, the mental and emotional demands on parents increase. Everyone recognizes that raising a child places strain on the person with this responsibility—which is why even secular courts work to ensure that single parents have financial and other practical support from former spouses. In a Christian marriage, God has built in the blessing of having each other to bear this responsibility together. Children place pressure on a marriage simply by their existence, and this is not a bad thing. It forces a couple to lean on each other more fully as they team up to raise their children in the fear and admonition of the Lord. Is there a mother with preschoolers (or teenagers) who has not said, "Go to your room until your father gets home!"? The ability to have a break while a spouse takes over for a bit, the opportunity to discuss how a child is doing and how to guide him or her, the chance to encourage each other in this crucial task does enable us to continue, and to find blessing as we do. The support of a spouse as a coparent can be an incredibly affirming and joyful thing. Sometimes pressure is a privilege: in a Christian marriage, the labor of coparenting is often a joyful one.

Parents have the joint responsibility of steering their children through a broken world, and while this can be hard—sometimes heartbreaking—God has given blessing even here. The ability to go into a dark bedroom where a nightmare has brought terror and instead to bring safety and peace is a privilege. Sitting up late together in a living room, listening to a teenager wrestle with job difficulties, is a road that we get to walk. Helping each other run a home as sickness moves through creates a place for rest and recovery. Being there as an example of faithful joy in the aftermath of a college student's breakup provides a rock for the child to lean on. Holding a child's hand—at any age—by a graveside is the blessing of bringing comfort and words of resurrection hope. Wiping away tears of all sorts is a small reflection of God's removal of our own griefs as we enter glory (Rev. 21:4). Partnership of this sort brings blessing as husband and wife share the responsibility and respect that comes from leading our little ones through darkness, and providing comfort and safety in the valleys.

But parents also have the double joy of showing their children beauty. Bringing them to see the ocean, tending a garden, visiting a museum, climbing a mountain, listening to music—there are more ways to enjoy beauty with our children than there is time. When one of our children was born, friends gave us a card that said, "Enjoy showing her God's beautiful world." That is a good way to think about parenting. The privilege of introducing another person to God's beautiful works in this world is one that brings joy to fathers and mothers who have this blessing.

Christian parents also get the blessing of bringing their children into the church. The presence of children puts pressure on a marriage that goes far beyond sleep deprivation, and though God has created husband and wife to be a parental team, the primary source of teaching, care, and love for children, our children need more than we can ever give them. While children do place pressure on a marriage—and that is often a good thing because it pushes spouses closer—the fallenness of this world and its people means that sometimes that pressure becomes damaging. Busy seasons and ordinary feelings of being overwhelmed, as well as chronic illness, disability, and large spiritual issues—these sorts of things create burdens too big for a couple. They were meant for a community, and God has given the church for these things.

There are also limits to parental ability and wisdom: we cannot teach our children everything, support them all the time, or allow the role of parent to swallow up other biblical responsibilities. When it comes to bringing up children, "the Christian faith adds to the burden."[3] Raising children in Christ has challenges that pagan parents do not face. We are not simply called to teach them reading, writing, arithmetic, social skills, and sports. We are called to teach them God Himself. Certainly, this is beyond parents, even if they are very capable people. There is blessedness in being able to bring children to a place where they have the care and resources of a community, to be raised "within the covenant of grace, in faith, not fear."[4] Other believing adults create positive accountability in classrooms, encouragement in homes, and resources of all kinds for our children: God gives us the experience and wisdom of a community as an incredible resource to tap into. It helps to maintain the sanity of a marriage.

In a good church, our children are also able to develop healthy relationships that will bless them in ways that we cannot. They visit other Christian homes and see the gospel lived out in different family cultures. They see other personalities working out differences and enjoying blessings. We are not meant to parent alone. Ingrafting our family into the church family takes unnecessary pressure off a marriage.

But the privilege of bringing children into the church extends beyond helping a marriage. It also multiplies the joy that parents have.

Having the support, love, and wisdom of the church family as we work together to raise our children is invaluable. It goes far beyond baby showers and postpartum meals, which in themselves give space for recovery and family bonding. Bringing our children into the community of believers means covenantal care as they grow. It gives them the Word and sacraments. It provides a stable community. It means that prayers that we do not yet know to pray are made on their behalf by older saints. It shows our children—and us—what embodied faithfulness looks like as we see other saints walking faithfully in their own stages of life. We may and must "bring our children into the total environment of the Christian fellowship, so that prayer as well as worship and study becomes second nature [significant phrase!] to them."[5] There is deep blessing in bringing our children to Jesus' house and people. Being a church-integrated family allows us to help our children form connections, develop relationships, and find role models who will be there for them when we cannot be, and especially when we no longer are.

And God has provided happiness simply in sharing with those people. There is joy in telling an older couple what the toddler said and enjoying their laughter. There is blessing in watching a college student hold a baby for the first time. It is a happy thing to see a child filling up at a fellowship meal, taking in good food as well as the atmosphere that he or she is not yet aware of. Parenting in the context of the church brings blessing in the practicalities as well as the intangibles of life.

This is part of the reason that, in the church, covenant children are a blessing to marriages beyond their parents'. Couples without their own children can still enjoy the children in the church. One childless couple we knew were incredible at ministering to and enjoying other people's children as they babysat, taught new skills, read books out loud, helped with meals, and even delivered a baby who arrived in a hurry. This couple loved to get to know, teach, and laugh with the children that God had given them in the church. Children in a church bring happiness to many more adults than Mom and Dad. The church also bears a covenantal responsibility for them, and finding ways to both enjoy and care for these little ones can bring real blessing to a couple to whom God has not given their own children.

But there are also deeply personal and private aspects to having children. One of these is painful: watching our own sins manifested in a little person whom we love. Very often, children demonstrate propensities to sin that they inherited along with a personality and physical features. Early on, they reflect the atmosphere of their home, including idiosyncratic weaknesses. While this is hard for Christian parents to watch and live with, it can actually bear fruit in a marriage. Seeing your own sins clearly in a son or daughter whom you love can give you a glimpse into what your spouse lives with. A child's behavior can be a mirror held up right in front of you, forcing you to confront things in yourself that you would not otherwise see. By the Spirit, a believer will be able to respond to this with repentance to a spouse and renewed desire to fight against his or her own sin. Sometimes children bring joy to a marriage by forcing a couple to grow in humility and creating a desire for specific sanctification.

A marriage can also be strengthened by children as a couple learns about different personalities and backgrounds from each other. Perhaps you have a daughter who is not like you or your spouse: she is like a grandmother, and you get to learn about a totally new personality and set of strengths and interests. This might not seem appealing, but it is an avenue of growth, and one that synchronizes with knowledge and experience that your spouse already has.

Children, for all the fun and happiness, can bring you to an end in yourself. Is there a mother who has not cried about her inadequacy, or a father who has not felt frustration at an inability to fix things for or in a child? Even with a good church, even working as a team, we will regularly come to the end of our abilities. Children bring us to the Lord again and again. They actually push us closer to Him, and as they unknowingly do, we are able to more clearly see the Lord as our own heavenly Father and go to Him as His beloved children with all our needs.

But the blessing of a happy marriage is not only for the couple. Children who grow up with parents who enjoy each other and are joyful together have a context of security and love in which to thrive. As the people impacted the most outside the marriage itself, children are massively affected by the condition of the parents' relationship. A happy marriage is one of the greatest gifts that a couple can give to their children, and parents who are happy in each other are a lifelong blessing to children who grow up absorbing a happy home atmosphere.

The Reformer Martin Bucer and his wife Elizabeth had eleven children together. Though they knew the effects of sin in their family, and ended up burying nearly all of their sons and daughters, the joy that these young souls brought is clear in Bucer's writing. He argued that for believers, having children was a multiplication of love: the husband and wife's physical love for each other creating more people in the home to love and more people in the home to love one another. It was a compound loving and being loved.

But it is a love, according to the Lord's covenantal faithfulness, that carries forward through time. This idea should bring great happiness to parents as well as the church community: Christian love carries forward in time through covenant children. The multigenerational structure that God created as normative is designed not only for love and happiness in our own family and generation but also as a vehicle to carry that covenantal love and joy forward in time: "Posterity shall serve him; it shall be told of the Lord to the coming generation; they shall come and proclaim his righteousness to a people yet unborn, that he has done it" (Ps. 22:30–31). Part of the happiness of a Christian marriage is parenting in faith, "so that a people yet to be created may praise the Lord" (Ps. 102:18), bringing our little family into the great, time-spanning, globe-circling family of God. We can do this without presumption because it is something that God both describes and promises in His Word: "They shall be the offspring of the blessed of the Lord, and their descendants with them" (Isa. 65:23). God's plan is that "the father makes known to the children [His] faithfulness" (38:19). The joy for Christian parents is both in proclamation and in seeing the Lord be faithful to His promise of being a God not only to us but also to our children.

Whether the Apostle John was referencing actual children or a congregation, his words resonate with believing mothers and fathers: "I have no greater joy than to hear that my children are walking in the truth" (3 John 4) because it means that our earthly families have joined the eternal one and can enjoy the happiness of salvation together. Perhaps this is why one of the most beautiful benedictions in the Old Testament involves this covenantal line: "May you live to see your children's children! Peace be upon Israel!" (Ps. 128:6).

Story (2007)

Charles and Abigail grew up in the same church. They started talking after Charles emailed Abigail while she was working in Europe and said that he missed her—which she thought was weird because they had not talked much when she was home. They started dating when Abigail returned. She knew it was for real because Charles was so guarded and standoffish toward friendship with women at church and at the young-adult Bible study that they were in. They were married in 2007 and live in the Midwest countryside.

Do you have a happy marriage?

Mostly, yes.

How do you know that?

Mostly we're happy and sometimes we're not. We've decided to have a happy marriage and made it a priority.

How have you done that?

Having the foundation and rhythm of church (Sunday rest) and the weekly structures around it (like prayer meeting) and times together are essential. So is humility. Happiness takes work. Healthy habits like eating well, getting exercise, being disciplined, good conversation, sex, and enough sleep definitely help. Personal devotions, listening to God and His Word, are necessary. Listening, hearing, patient waiting for answers to prayer. Treating God like He exists.

Has your marriage always been happy?

No.

What are some things that your marriage has overcome to be at the place that it is now?

Barrenness, family-business struggles, difficult interpersonal relationships in family, spiritual abuse, and overcoming selfishness in learning how to care for each other.

How did you cope with barrenness together?

We decided not to pursue untested, experimental procedures that the doctor was offering in response to recurring miscarriages. We felt that the doctor was excited to use us as a test case, and that was a turnoff. We waited; we prayed. We are in a church culture that values family and motherhood, so that was especially hard for Abigail. So we prayed and waited, thinking that maybe God wanted us not to have children. I [Abigail] found other things to fill my time: teaching, training horses, home life. We also found a new church home and met a family who had also walked through this. They had a healthy family and healthy view of adoption. We talked with them a lot. That was especially encouraging to Charles. Church life (especially sermons and fellowship) increased our stability, relationally and spiritually. We decided to start the adoption process as I [Abigail] was still "not over it" after six or seven years of childlessness. We trusted that God would stop us in the adoption process by closing the door if that was His will. God opened the door for two adoptions, and when we started to think about a third adoption, we prayed and waited again and were unsure. Whenever we are unsure of something, we wait and continue life as it is until direction is more clear. So we waited. Our third child was born to us biologically. Looking back, God has led every step. Now we are very busy, but waiting and open to what God might have us do in the future.

What things have you found that detract from happiness in your marriage?

Selfishness, distractions, overwork, lack of care and concern for each other—thoughtlessness. Lack of clear communication, too.

How do you deal with remaining sin in yourselves in marriage?

Forgive when asked, and when you sin, repent to the other person that you sinned against. Pray, go to church, read the Bible. Remember that Jesus sees the sin, too, and turn to Him. It frees you up not to be your spouse's savior. Stress management is important, too. Care for physical felt needs. Encourage and support each other. Make sure the other person knows that they don't fight alone and point them to Jesus. Listen to the other person: maybe they just need to talk.

What things have you noticed that drain happiness?

Stress, sin (each other's and other people's), lack of reflection, excessive noise, lack of sleep, relationships with ungodly people.

Who are your marriage role models?

Our parents by default because we are closest to them, but we take the good and leave the bad. We can observe the fruit of the decisions that our parents made as directly related to the churches they were/are part of and how that impacted their parenting and lifestyles. Grandparents are similarly role models. Abraham and Sarah, Hannah and Elkanah, Ruth and Boaz, too, because they are biblical examples.

Why those couples from the Bible? There are many you could have chosen; what made you pick these?

It seems like most of the biblical examples generally experienced barrenness. We looked at how Sarah's bitterness led her to make rash, unbiblical decisions with Hagar. But then later the New Testament shows Sarah in her sanctification, highlighting her faith in God and ability to submit to Abraham even in his foolish decisions. Hannah and Elkanah because of barrenness. Elkanah loved Hannah and served the church even in the midst of such awful, wicked leadership under Eli's sons. He didn't give up on serving the Lord or his wife just because the situation was horrible, and neither did Hannah. Hannah brought her petitions to the Lord in His house (however poorly run) and felt dismissed. With Boaz and Ruth, it's the self-sacrifice, devotedness to God and His ways. Samson and Delilah as well, as a warning example: this is what happens when you go after "felt" needs—lust—and indulge in worldliness. Delilah shows how to ruin a man with her femininity and sex appeal, this place that is supposed to be private, sacred, and full of trust. And yet God gives him grace. Samson and Delilah are a picture of what not to do.

Can you share one story or event that shaped or shifted your relationship, or made you think differently about it or your spouse?

Abigail: Seeing Charles interact kindly, graciously, and firmly with our children's birth parents. He treats them with dignity while simultaneously protecting our family and my fragile heart, especially at times when I can't handle things emotionally anymore.

Charles: Seeing Abigail have a difficult miscarriage while we were traveling. Seeing her in pain and weakness—dying, in a way—and nothing I could do about it.

How do you live with sadness in a good marriage?

It's part of life, as Westley says in *The Princess Bride*: "Life is pain, Highness. Anyone who says differently is selling something." It's helpful not to have a "happily ever after" mentality about marriage and life in general. When there is sadness, we cry together, cling to each other, read the Bible together. Counseling from a trusted, qualified person helps.

How has barrenness shaped your marriage?

Not being able to have children for several years helped us cling together in a nondistracted way. We know what it is to be low and high. We know what it is to hold a child and to lose them. We see Jesus taking care of us through it all, and it gives us deepened faith in Him.

What has your marriage been able to do because it is happy?

We can speak the truth to each other and still be one.

What has been the fruit of your marriage outside of your happiness?

Hospitality is a big one. Self-sacrifice, peace, the ability to cultivate healthy outside interests and meaningful friendships outside of our marriage, too.

What encouragement would you give to someone in an unhappy marriage?

To another Christian? Surround yourself with godly men and women. Don't give up, don't do it alone, seek the good, seek outside help, pray, wait. Encourage, encourage, encourage. Don't suffer alone. Keep going to Sunday worship. Share with people who will pray to Jesus on your behalf. Fight for the other person; fight for your spouse's joy and don't stop.

What is your favorite thing about being married?

Abigail: I am not alone. The goodness, peace, and safety.

Charles: I have companionship and a heritage. Having a home and not a house.

5

Accountability

If we say we have fellowship with him while we walk in darkness, we lie and do not practice the truth. But if we walk in the light, as he is in the light, we have fellowship with one another, and the blood of Jesus his Son cleanses us from all sin.

—1 John 1:6–7

Accountability is not the most comfortable word. We can think of it as code for confrontation or conflict, loss of privacy or autonomy. But instead of being a negative thing that only minors or irresponsible adults have, accountability is something that every human needs. We are all prone to wander, prone to go our own way, because we cannot see ourselves or our circumstances clearly. We need people around us who love us enough to kindly and carefully point out things that are damaging us—including us. This is especially true when we are unaware or unalarmed about issues because sin, as Jim Elliot wrote, "saps animation (Ps. 37:20) as cancer."[1] Sin will suck the life out of you and your marriage. Accountability seeks to prevent that.

On one level, accountability is the gift of someone who loves you pointing out something that is hurting you. It is being called back to safety. This is part of the reason that admitting, commiserating about, sympathizing with, or simply reviewing sins over coffee is not accountability. Accountability is the responsibility that believers have of sacrificially being our brother's keeper for his good. It is self-sacrificing because it willingly cares at a personal cost. The concerned observations of a believing spouse are a significant aid to holiness. When God puts you in a Christian marriage, He puts you in a context that allows the exposure of your sin to the light of another Christian's view and prayer and support in the fight against sin. The level and nature of the accountability will, in a healthy marriage, match the level and expression of sin.

Accountability is not a one-way street. We not only receive correction and help, but we also have the responsibility of asking for it when we realize on our own that something is hurting us or we are hurting someone else. Accountability can be calling out for help to someone whose feet are on solid ground. The Apostle James tells us to confess our sins to each other (James 5:16). This is part of the responsibility of accountability. It is most necessary and appropriate in Christian marriage. Martin Bucer called Christian marriage "a special and significant school and workshop of faith."[2]

Because of this, biblical accountability is not given from a position of superior to inferior. When either spouse behaves as though he or she is spiritually superior, wielding moral power over the other, that is not accountability. When it becomes about building ourselves up and putting the other person down, that is not accountability. When it is one spouse venting about annoyances in the relationship, that is not accountability. When Christ's supreme authority over anyone or His image in anyone is diminished, then what is happening is not accountability. Accountability is not control or coercion or complaining. These things are abuse. Real accountability, like biblical church discipline, is never demeaning, harmful, or belittling. It is a helping hand to a loved one who needs it, a shout of encouragement or warning, and an outreached hand to a fellow pilgrim who stumbles.

Even though believers are justified and saved, we are still sinners (2 Cor. 5:17). So right accountability might create temporary conflict, as we respond sinfully to biblical correction or respond biblically to sinful correction. When conflict does arise in a Christian marriage, there should always be the expectation of resolution—or freedom to disagree within biblical boundaries. Healthy accountability happens within the context of safety and Scripture's ultimate rule over our lives.

It still might be uncomfortable. Jordan Peterson offers insightful observations of unaddressed issues in a marriage. These almost always create distance or frustration: "Under such circumstances, there is nothing but a fight—a fight with peace as the goal—that will reveal the truth." While a fight is not inevitable for the Christian, conflict might come in between speaking the truth in love and renewed peace. Peterson continues, "Perhaps addressing that and (you never know) solving the problem would be worth . . . the misery just telling each other the truth (not with intent to destroy, or attain victory, because that's not the truth: that's just all-out war)."[3] A couple can have serious discussions or even confrontation and still be in fellowship with each other. If there is an awareness that this is an issue that they are trying to solve together, not something to throw back and forth at each other's heads, then raised voices, unkind words, or the silent treatment become redundant as well as sinful. But even without an actual fight, having a spouse address an issue is rarely comfortable. That is why people often avoid it. But avoidance is living in the short term with little regard for the long-term effects of the status quo. "Do you truly think it wise," Peterson asks, "to let the catastrophe grow in the shadows, while you shrink and decrease and become ever more afraid?"[4]

Afraid of what? Many things, depending partly on the health of your marriage, your personality, past experiences, and stress levels. But this fear to speak the truth often stems from wrong—often selfish—priorities. Amy Carmichael observed, "If I am afraid to speak the truth, lest I lose affection, or lest the one concerned should say, 'You do not understand,' or because I fear to lose my reputation for kindness; if I put my own good name before the other's highest good, then I know nothing of Calvary love."[5]

This does not mean that truth trumps kind words and care. We often function as though truth and kindness are at odds—perhaps because our sin often makes them look like enemies. We are called to kindness, including in confrontation. Sometimes a faithful spouse wounds (Prov. 27:6) as he or she kindly confronts, though never as one whose rash words are sword thrusts, but as one with a wise tongue that brings healing (12:18).

Accountability is more than wise confrontation. It is aimed at more than avoiding relational catastrophe and creating a better marriage. It is aimed at Christlikeness. In a Christian union, this accountability comes from someone who is publicly committed to you and whose thoughts are shaped by Scripture. Loving warnings and observations are essential. Difficult as the truth may be, when it is spoken in love from one Christian to another, it facilitates fellowship.

It removes obstacles—wrong ideas, unhealthy habits, sins—from between people, allowing them to be close to one another, bringing happiness.

While this is true for all relationships, it is especially true of a marriage simply because of the degree of intimacy. The barbs of self-centeredness and self-focus and self-obsession are broken off, are sanded down, and stop tearing at the fabric of relationships surrounding us. When iron sharpens iron, sparks can fly as metal is ground into a new shape. Things can get heated. But when this happens in the context of truth through biblical accountability, it is not friction that produces bitterness and warping. No, it wisely, kindly, and carefully removes things that are legitimately offensive to others—primarily our God—so that closeness can deepen. It allows a deeper intimacy, with the Lord, our spouse, and our neighbor. Biblical accountability fosters true maturity. It facilitates usefulness. It prepares for service.

When it is biblical, accountability has nothing to do with critique for critique's sake, ferreting out another's weakness, or going after a speck while we blink at our plank. Instead, biblical accountability is meek. In his discussion on meekness, Matthew Henry wrote that it is not weakness or being submissive to all strength or criticism. Instead, it is being lamblike in our own cause and lionlike in God's. This is why Scripture could describe Moses as the meekest of men: he was working and speaking out not for himself but for God and His people. Accountability in marriage needs to be set in a context of the meekness that all believers are called to but is particularly precious and useful in relationship with our spouses.

Meekness also provides a filter for us to evaluate what and when to address in our spouses: are we being lamblike in terms of our own wants and needs? Or, regardless of tone, is this actually about our being irritated or tired or fed up? Or are we seeing and addressing things from God's perspective for the good of our spouses, even at cost to ourselves? Carmichael commented, "If I can hurt another by speaking faithfully without much preparation of spirit, and without hurting myself far more than I hurt that other, then I know nothing of Calvary love."[6] Faithful speaking is never the only issue. As believers, we must be concerned not only with speaking what is true, but also with not speaking what is true in a way that cuts down, perpetuates our own sin, and does not seek our spouses' good.

Perhaps this is why understanding is just as much a part of accountability as meekness is. The Apostle specifically calls husbands to live in an understanding way with their wives, showing them honor instead of superiority, harshness, or scorn (1 Peter 3:7). Asking questions to make sure that we understand our spouses' behavior and words is simple wisdom. Addressing a perceived issue before we hear is shameful foolishness (Prov. 18:13). Accountability without humility is not Christian behavior. We are even told that "love covers a multitude of sins" (1 Peter 4:8). Christians are not to bring up others' weaknesses or sins unnecessarily or lightly, and the closer the relationship, the more this matters.

This is because biblical accountability within a marriage is an issue of morality. The goal of accountability and even confrontation is peace—peace not just with each other but also with the Lord. It is aimed at an alliance with your spouse, yes, but also with truth. This is what Psalm 119:165 comments on: "Great peace have those who love your law." That law—God's Word—is truth (John 17:17). So another way to think about accountability is as an undeceiving. Satan is always out to deceive, and our own sin blinds us, so clear vision for us and those around us is a gift. Often, our spouses are the first to be able to see where we are drifting from truth, bending away from "the straightedge of Scripture."[7] So for the believer, accountability is one aspect of truth-telling, truth-seeking, and truth-proclaiming. It is the ability to fellowship in the light of God's Word (Ps. 119:105). It is a way to fight lies.

After all, lies are the devil's language (John 8:44). It is love that rejoices in the truth (1 Cor. 13:6), and we are to speak that truth in love (Eph. 4:15). In our fallen condition, we are prone to live out different lies. Perhaps we are shaped by the lie that money will make us happy. Maybe we behave as though this tangible world were our lasting city. Perhaps we function under the illusion that we have control over life. There are many ways to be deceived, and so we need many undeceptions being called back to a way of life that is in line with our public confession. In healthy marriages, we have the joy of walking with spouses who are committed not only to our happiness, but also to the life of truth in us and the blessing that comes from that.

Part of the large cultural shift that the Protestant Reformation created was evident in marriage, and accountability proved to be a significant aspect of that newly biblical paradigm. Katharina Zell, author and wife of Reformer Matthew Zell, saw her husband first as a brother in Christ and second as a spouse, and so she was partly responsible for his spiritual safety as the Christian who was closest to him. Because spouses see what others cannot or do not, they are also hurt in ways that more distant people are not. They are also in a very particular place, uniquely designed to help us become undeceived, fight sin, and carry our cross (Matt. 16:24) in a way that other people cannot. The closeness of marriage itself brings a responsibility of merciful accountability for believers.

For Martin and Elizabeth Bucer, a mutual accountability included kind and godly criticism. After Elizabeth's death and his own remarriage, Bucer wrote, "[My new wife] is not as free in criticism as my first wife, and I now realize that such liberty is not only wholesome but necessary."[8] Like iron sharpening iron, Elizabeth's criticism shaped his work and ministry. It must have been done in love for both Bucer and the church, since it seems to have been part of the marriage's normal and healthy flow. It brought blessing not only to Bucer but also to his congregation. And it was done in a way that brought closeness, not division. A strong advocate of biblical leadership and submission, Bucer was known for his willingness to admit and renounce mistakes—something that surely made this marital give-and-take easier.[9] Perhaps Elizabeth's "necessary" criticism helped give a balance to his later ministry that his early, stormy years lacked. Such "wholesome" liberty is a good example of submission with backbone, but also of accountability that was for the good of the spouse and also brought the happiness of oneness.

Perhaps this is because, for a growing Christian, the best and strongest kind of accountability is simply the daily presence of another growing Christian. Good examples—even imperfect ones—are powerful. Did you ever have a teacher who made you want to learn simply because the teacher loved the subject and you as his or her student? Or a coach whose enthusiasm for the game and belief that you could do better gave you energy to excel? Christians do the same for each other. This is why some of the most effective accountability in the world is living with someone who is like Jesus. Not only a different personality, a different history, and a different perspective, but all of that shaped into a cruciform life is an embodied reminder of our Lord. Life with a spouse who is in love with Jesus is a calling back and undeceiving by example in word and deed. The beauty of holiness, especially manifested by loving sacrifice in a marriage, has incredible power to change a Christian spouse.

Even an imperfect embodiment of Christlikeness will, by the Spirit's power and in His timing, have a sanctifying effect on a spouse. It might be conscious or otherwise, but just as living with sin will have an effect, so will living with godliness. In Exodus 29:43, God speaks of the sanctifying effect of His visible glory in the tabernacle. The very presence of God's holiness in the camp had a spiritual effect on the people. When, by grace, that same glory is manifested in the life of a husband or wife, a believing spouse will be blessed and encouraged to pursue Jesus more fervently. Seeing God's glory in and through a Christian partner will create an accountability that is welcome and beautifying because it honors the Lord who gives it as it makes us more like Jesus. As we see in others aspects of Christlikeness that we lack and that we are enabled by the Spirit to pursue, real repentance, real change, and real fellowship deepen, often without a human word.

A powerful earthly picture of Christ's love for me is a love that persists even in the face of my sins and shortcomings and does not tire of forgiveness and patience and the relationship itself. You might ask why a godly spouse still loves you and puts up with you and wants to be with you despite being hurt by you, seeing your daily weakness and deep need of grace. There really is not any reason in us! Christian love is out of proportion to our lovability. It is a reflection of God's love for His people, whom He loves simply because He does. You cannot help but be transformed by such a love. Just as Christ's love for His people transforms them, so the love of a godly husband or wife transforms a spouse. Living with a love that is generous and consistent and sacrificial is a love that, for the Christian, creates a desire to be worthy of it. That is the best accountability there is, and though there may be gentle and careful "wounds of a friend" when needed, this is an accountability that cannot be distinguished from love because it is love. This sort of Christlike life will be its own accountability.

That is why biblical accountability has no belittling or berating, no nagging or pushing, no condescension or superiority. It will be like the love of Jesus, facilitating holiness, quiet (Zeph. 3:17), safety, and a zeal for further union, especially with the Lord. It will largely be building one another up, encouragement in holiness, and prayer for the Spirit's presence and work in each other. God knows that we need this in the Christian life, and He often provides it wonderfully through marriages that are centered on Him.

If you have seen or experienced this sort of presence in a marriage, you know the happiness that it brings: trust, harmony, humility, and blessing. Biblical accountability in a marriage of believers looks far less like sympathizing with similar struggles at a coffee shop than it does like Jesus' sacrificial love. The goal of accountability is John the Baptist's prayer: "He must increase, but I must decrease" (John 3:30). The happiness of accountability is the same thing. It is a conscious subjugation of pride and self, which always bring misery, to Christ's lordship, which always produces joy in the believer.

Story (2002)

Jim and Lisa's marriage has been shaped by three countries, many career changes, multiple children, serious health issues, disability, and more. These answers come largely through Lisa's voice but are from both of them.

Do you have a happy marriage?

Yes. We genuinely enjoy being together and seek each other's company. We laugh together, pray together, share freely the deepest thoughts to the simplest daily stuff of life. We value each other's thoughts and perspectives, and there is a mutual respect for each other as individuals. We've also had times of conflict and unhappiness, particularly in the earlier years of marriage, and know what it means to work toward oneness and happiness.

Has your marriage always been happy?

Marriage has not been a static happy experience for us, but a growing relationship with seasons of disappointment and joy mixed together. And as each marriage is made of two individuals, people can have a different experience of the same relationship. Some of it is a difference in personality, expectation, the marriage norms we have in mind, and an understanding of what marriage and love are. While Jim would describe our marriage as always happy, I experienced loneliness and disappointment in the early years that I never felt free to share with anyone. Had we failed? Did I marry the wrong person? Where do we go from here? After all, the marriage counseling we had was one session, and the couple shared that they never fought and enjoyed a marriage of mutual love and happiness. So when we wrestled, I told no one. But by God's grace, the Holy Spirit over many years and steady sanctification matured us both emotionally and spiritually.

What things have you found that detract from happiness in your marriage?

Sin is the biggest detractor of happiness. That's the umbrella term, but truly—personal holiness brings relational happiness. Holiness allows you to live for something or someone bigger than yourself.

Selfishness and pettiness are massive detractors, while sacrificial and generous love that covers minor irritations and annoyances can bring life and renewal to the most stagnant of marriages. Courtesy matters. Respect matters and is often a prerequisite to love—it means we don't take each other for granted but realize the personhood of each other and the gift it is to cherish and build a life together. God has a good work to do in one another, and often we are the person that gets to be in the front-row seat of that and a chief tool in it (that means it can be painful, and persistence and hope are essential!).

What are some things that your marriage has overcome to be at the place that it is now?

Conflict. We've learned how to communicate well, and it has helped us come to a point of something like this: Both agree that we want the best for our marriage. That God calls us to continual sanctification. We want to grow our marriage and not turn it into a complacent, bitter, or unengaged relationship. Marriage is not static because we are two dynamic people who will go through many circumstances and seasons in life. When there's conflict, we first align ourselves with these realities: we both want a good marriage, to honor the Lord, and to show respect and love for each other. That governs the way we speak and engage. No one has the right to inflict emotional pain by raised voices, pettiness, silent treatment, walking off, or exaggeration. But instead, deal honestly and in a spirit of mutuality with one another and before the Lord. This requires humility on both parts, and a mutual commitment. With this posture, conflict is the ironing out of bumps that still exist and need to be worked on. But on the other side is greater understanding, growth, and maturity.

Tragedy. I say tragedy, because that's what comes to mind with the intense losses when Luke was first born. The emotional pain of watching the suffering of a child is isolating and, even though you are in it together, can affect two people differently. Jim's unwavering love for me and Luke was, and continues to be, one of the greatest gifts of my life. We both processed things differently and struggled spiritually, and I almost had a complete breakdown. Although there were times of relational challenges in it, through it all, Jim's love was constant and brought comfort and stability, and made the pain more bearable. At the lowest low, he loved me and was present in every way. God also used the tragedy to bring a lot of healing to areas of our relationship, probably because it brought rapid maturation in many areas. In many ways, it was a spiritual and relational "greenhouse" by God's grace, even though it felt like a desert.

Financial struggle. With life upended, we lost everything. Every dime we had saved was quickly gone in the first year to cover Luke's medical care. We lived in a rundown rental house, and once Jim had his permanent residency, he began teaching but made a salary that was not livable. He started doing some work on the side and tried to grow it to a small business. It meant twelve- to fourteen-hour days with me carrying the weight of everything at home: nurses in our house, Luke's endless appointments, and the other three kids at that time. I remember my mom bringing groceries at one point, and I felt so humiliated. We wanted to be the helpers, not the ones to be helped. We felt trapped in a corner—so many people build a career within the first decade of married life, which sets the trajectory for the rest of their lives. We had been on the mission field and now had to start over at square one with circumstances that felt impossible. Our peers were in nice homes, taking great vacations, while I was trying to figure out how to make groceries stretch on $65 a week. I was too proud to use any government help and promised myself I would figure out a solution before depending on anyone else. Eventually the business did well and Luke became more stable, giving us more bandwidth to care for our family financially. It did drive me to finish school (which was also a huge outlet for me) and start working, which provided a ton of relief for our family, especially as Jim started seminary. We have deep empathy for people struggling to manage the rest of life during health crises. Life doesn't stop, and bills need to be paid even when you're flat on your back from illness and tragedy. It can be a huge stressor on a marriage, and individually it is very difficult to feel like a burden to others, the church, and society. I think that's what drives us now to give generously with whatever God gives us:

whether finances, our home, our ability to physically work, a mind that is clear and able. Everything we have is a gift from Him.

How do you deal with remaining sin in yourselves in marriage?

With hope. When you journey on in sanctification in life, you learn to have growing hope. The Lord never wants to leave us in our sin, but continues to transform us as we look to Christ. I believe this for my spouse. I believe this for me! And this is the basis of my prayers: "Continue your work in us, Lord. Make us useful and beautiful. Don't leave us this way!" Sin distorts our humanity, while Christlikeness brings life and healing to us individually, our marriage, and the community around us.

With realism. Sin will be part of us and our marriage on earth. The degree and nature matters, but we need to be prepared and equipped. Be in prayer with one another. Be honest before the Lord with the secret sins in our hearts. Live an examined life: "Lord, show me. Lead me. Deliver me. Restore us. Keep us." Having experienced joy in relationship, the freedom of a clean conscience, and the devastating domino effects of sin is a strong deterrent from engaging in personal sinful habits, thoughts, actions. Quick confession and acknowledgment to one another and the Lord creates a culture that is resistant to the creeping nature of sin.

With wisdom. While we cannot expect perfection, we should expect a steady growth in each other as followers of Christ. Are we growing more selfish or self-giving? More petty or more gracious? Self-controlled, or do desires rule us? We cannot nag each other into holiness, but we can nurture it through personal godliness and together pursuing Christ. As spouses, we have tremendous influence on one another's growth and godliness. If the spouse is not interested, much prayer and wisdom is needed. It's a great sorrow for many when one person is invested and the other not. Marry in the Lord!

What things have you noticed that drain happiness? Are there any habits or patterns that establish/perpetuate happiness?

A lack of respect and love displayed by pettiness, selfishness, and a lack of courtesy. Manners matter. Do we make room for the other person and show honor for their whole person? We have the possibility to grow strong and healthy relationships when both desire to build up and nurture the other through the simple, everyday things of life.

The desire to control one another is a sure way to frustrated efforts and resentment of both parties. There is a tension with realizing that each person is their own individual and allowing freedom for that while also realizing that each person's actions affect the relationship and even the way you as a couple relate to others around you. Careful encouragement may be needed while avoiding the traps of micromanagement, the desire to be seen a certain way by others, or being a defeating force to your spouse. Allow freedom for individuality between the boundaries of a healthy marriage.

Happiness is also perpetuated when we allow the other person to grow. See each person as unique with their own ideas, gifts, hobbies, interests. Be invested in their growth and delight. We find a lot of joy in exploring together—be it on a road trip to a Podunk town or intellectually with ideas! Realize that the other person is dynamic and has the capacity to change and grow and flourish. Work toward mutual flourishing as you follow Christ. This makes aging exciting: who will we be in twenty years? We hope that we will have discovered new dimensions and deeper joy of marriage, of life, and in following the Lord.

Who are your marriage role models? Why?

We've seen things we admire in couples and cobbled together our own hopes from examples around us. In many ways, it's been principles exemplified that have really shaped us. For example, a missionary couple that highly valued children and excelled in educating them at home and raising them with strong leadership principles. Or the couple that exemplifies faithfulness—a man who visits his wife daily as she suffers from severe dementia at a young age. The couple at church that always speaks highly of one another and shows honor to each other in the big and little things of life. The list goes on! In all, recognizing biblical principles alive and thriving in the lives of those around us.

How do you live with sadness in a good marriage?

A good question. A good marriage recognizes the changing seasons to one event or situation. People process differently, and experience grief differently and to varying degrees in any given season. We learned to communicate and share through it all. Helping us understand one another and the ways we were coping. For Jim, it was working nonstop; for me, I went through significant anxiety and depression. We constantly recalibrated ourselves to the promises of God and the character of God, helping each other feel their way across what seemed like an eternal abyss to resting in the Lord.

We built in lightheartedness where we could. In some seasons, we needed just a moment of relief. Which meant watching a great docuseries together, popping popcorn, a coffee-shop date, sharing fires on the patio. Jim would have humor or bring me a coffee, make a wry remark. Just little bright spots that made me laugh in a season of many tears. The whole family learned to rejoice together, cry together, and realize spiritual truths together.

We allowed space for each other. I would encourage Jim to take a few days away and go fishing. I took the kids one by one on a trip. We give each other permission to, without guilt, step away and be refreshed.

There is something very special about experiencing loss together. I wish it upon no one, but what a gift it is to be both so invested together in a child and to share the burden of unrealized dreams and devastating loss. A shared grief has knit us together in powerful ways and uniquely positions us to enjoy and sorrow over the things of life together. We both have gone through seasons of intense physical/emotional exhaustion and have learned how to care for each other at low points.

Jim is also very good about intentionally focusing on us as a couple, apart from our identity as parents or as special-needs parents. He wants us to be whole people, not identified as special-needs parents but just Lisa and Jim who love each other, their kids, and the Lord. We've tried to normalize our lives and live as whole people who have hard parts of life, but also very rich and blessed lives.

In time, sadness is tempered by reframing reality with the hope of the gospel—this is not the end. And also by the reality that many people suffer. We are not the only ones, but join a long line of humanity that has endured many difficult things. In Christ, this is not wasted, and it helps to realize that there is kingdom work we get to be a part of because of the circumstances we have and the ability to understand a different and ongoing level of grief.

How have "complicating factors" shaped your marriage?

A complicating factor would be exhaustion, medical emergency, and twenty-four-hour caregiving. It drains a person emotionally, but when physical resources are constantly depleted, it leaves you in a state with little to offer the other person. It is harder to look to the needs of the other when your own needs require desperate attention not just for well-being, but for surviving. Getting enough sleep to function, trying to get enough relief to get your body out of constant stress mode, etc. It's very difficult when both people are very depleted and the situation is chronic. It can lead to both persons' feeling uncared for, with romance a distant dream, and a relationship can shrink without its proper care and attention. I remember Jim saying in the early years of Luke, "I just miss my wife." I felt no time or energy to even care. Over time, we sharpened our communication; we would take shifts, which would allow the other person at least some rest, alternate nights, etc. There was also a lot of apologizing for words spoken out of frustrated exhaustion. The challenge was not having an end in sight. With a newborn, you know that things will trend toward regulation. With special needs, there's no end in sight to caring for the needs and constant dysregulation: that can be overwhelming. "Will I ever sleep again? Will I ever feel joy at waking up in the morning? I wish I could end this endless nightmare." We have become aware of our individual limits and, as we have added care to the home, have been much better able to work within those.

These days, a cup of coffee on a quiet morning is like a gift from heaven, literally! It's a gift to have an evening when the other spouse says, "You go to bed and I'll do Luke's care." There are a thousand tasks a day to be done, and so we both try to be mindful of the other's load. Having in-home nursing was another huge blessing and adjustment. A blessing because it relieves the load of care and helps us to be refreshed by doing other work. An adjustment because there is no place to call your own. Your home and space are always occupied, another person entering many of your conversations, and a lack of privacy that can leave you wanting to retreat, but the only place to retreat to is outside, which works only half the year when you live as far north as we do!

All of these situations have made us learn to be very adaptable and to just deal with whatever the day brings. We know our limits, we understand our needs, and we both seek to responsibly care for our own needs and look out for the other. This does mean a lot less time enjoying other things in life together, as leaving home together to go anywhere always involves logistics and making sure that Luke has care. We miss being able to do many things together and have to take solo vacations with the kids. Sometimes that's a real disappointment, but we try not to focus on that.

What has your marriage been able to do because it is happy? What has been the fruit of your marriage outside of your happiness?

I think the happiness of our marriage has spilled over to our children. We've had a very chaotic decade-plus; however, the commitment and mutual love and respect in our relationship has certainly affected the steadiness and atmosphere of the home. I think it has made our home a happy place, most days. Our children have learned many painful realities and disappointments, but parents who follow the Lord have the capacity to normalize joy and life in the middle of hard things.

Happiness in marriage also gives emotional bandwidth to invest in others' happiness. If marriage is generally a place of contentment and renewal, one can be working from a threshold of having their own relational needs largely met and, out of that, being able to share in others' needs. Happiness in marriage has an energizing effect on the rest of life and those around you. It has a compounding effect. I think we are able to be a source of comfort and encouragement to those who come to us.

It has also given us a lot of energy and desire to work together, outside our four walls. We love to work on projects together, particularly with the church in mind. It brings energy and joy to be planning our denomination's youth camp, participating in church life, and serving the church.

What encouragement would you give to someone in an unhappy marriage?

People are dynamic and not static. Even the most happy of marriages may experience seasons of deep disappointment and unhappiness. A marriage is made up of two people who come together, often on different growth trajectories. Marriage is these two diverse people coming together, and it takes time and work to build something together. Some people seem to do this effortlessly, but for others it can be a faithful pursuit. We can be sure that even this works for our own growth and godliness even if disappointment is very real.

Practically, there are many things you can work faithfully at regardless of how unhappy you feel: learn how to communicate and engage productively, be other-person-centered while growing your own person (what is it like to be married to me?!), create a shared vision of marriage together, and cultivate daily joy and courtesy.

Saturate your marriage with good things: biblical teaching, regular fellowship with godly friends, praying/talking/reading together. In times of disappointment (not from sin, but maybe missed expectations), focus on how God is calling you to grow, examine your expectations, try love and grace, and don't fix your joy solely on any person other than Christ.

If there is serious sin by you or your spouse, like lying, pornography, or anger, don't gloss over it or think you're being a better spouse by dismissing it. Dismissing enables it and is not noble. Exposure is the only way to begin repentance, restoration, and healing before God and one another. Hidden things just fester and destroy individuals and relationships. Involve godly counsel, whether it is someone from your church, your parents, or the elders if needed.

Although marriage can be very fulfilling, don't expect marriage alone to fill you. Instead, seek to live a full and meaningful life and bring that to your marriage. These are not easy fixes, but a lifelong posture that invites relational health.

What is your favorite thing about being married?

Companionship. There is nothing like having someone to share conversation with, dinner with, life with, whom you genuinely enjoy. Although I get to travel with my job, it honestly is half the delight it would be if I could experience it alongside Jim. I love seeing and experiencing the world with him. His laughter intensifies mine. My responses impact his. I give him ideas; he weeds them out and keeps the good ones. We serve together. Plan together. Parent together.

6

Safety

They shall dwell securely, and none shall make them afraid.
—Ezekiel 34:28

In 1523, a wagonload of nuns came to Wittenberg, Germany. The women had been converted out of Roman Catholicism, were fleeing their convent, and, Martin Luther wrote, arrived in town "more eager for marriage than for life."[1] Marriage meant financial security. It meant a place in society, provision, and physical protection. It meant safety.

Our culture is less dangerous than Europe was five hundred years ago: the West has more freedoms, legal protections, opportunities, and rights; it has fewer highwaymen, less powerful popes, and scarce abject poverty. But safety is still necessary for a marriage to flourish. It is also part of the design. God has created marriage to be a place of safety. And it is multifaceted. In his commentary on Genesis 2:18, Matthew Henry touched on several aspects: "That the woman was made from the rib he had taken out of man; not made out of his head to rule over him, nor out of his feet to be trampled on by him, but out of his side to be equal with him, under his arm to be protected, and near his heart to be beloved."[2] Physical, financial, emotional, relational, and spiritual safety are facets of this design feature, and each contributes to a happy marriage.

Safety is often, at root, an issue of self-control—an unnatural virtue that is on the decline in the West. A lack of self-control naturally comes with issues of anger, uncontrolled spending, verbal abuse, and many other problems that threaten the safety that God designed to be a blessing in marriage. Because self-control is increasingly rare in our post-Christian culture, the happiness that comes with safety in marriage is taking a serious hit. And this is one reason that Christian marriages will increasingly stand out as places of safety and refuge.

This does not mean that married Christians are immune to danger. A fallen world is not a safe place, and even in a healthy marriage, things can intrude into the safety of a happy relationship. Things such as financial disaster, accidents, thefts, and unkind words can breach the wall of safety that a good marriage should be. But though this is true, God designed safety in Christian marriage to be a thing that is not only real but also increasing. Outside circumstances might be dangerous and our sin can damage this refuge, but we can still experience the joy of refuge that a Christian marriage provides.

Perhaps this will be especially evident sexually. The covenant of marriage itself creates safety in a sexual relationship, establishing boundaries around it. This is safety both of kind, by a public commitment to each other, and also of permanence, because that commitment is to be lifelong. It is the safety of having healthy boundaries established and reinforced. It is the safety of exclusivity. Jim Elliot wrote of his fiancée in his journal: "I want my need to be always of *her*, not merely of *woman*—that would lead to awful temptation."[3] When our sexual need is always directed toward our spouses, it brings the joy of safety from temptation.

The Apostle Paul understood this and explained that it is better to marry than to burn (1 Cor. 7:9). The Book of Common Prayer clearly states that one of the biblical reasons for marriage is "for a remedy against sin, and to avoid fornication; that such persons as be married, might live chastlye in matrimony, and keep themselves undefiled members of Christ's body."[4] God has given marriage as a safe place for sexual activity: a context that is loving, happy, and protected.

There are physical consequences to this sexual safety—or lack of it. In a world where sexually transmitted diseases are becoming epidemics, the safety of healthy, biblical sex is increasingly clear. Visit any university campus and read a bulletin board to see resources for dealing with sexual disease and reminders to protect yourself against it. Part of the beauty of going to bed with a faithful spouse is freedom from these kinds of burdens: freedom from the fears and worries that come with rejection of God's design. It is the safety of health and protection from disease. Yes, there are Christians whose pasts mean that they will have consequences from promiscuity, who will have to be wise and careful: Scripture is honest about our pasts without being cold or judgmental (1 Cor. 6:11). But for most believers who come from a Christian background, this aspect of safety is there, and it brings great blessing.

The happiness of a safe sexual relationship was emphasized by a scene that my husband and I witnessed on our way to an event. Driving past a large hospital complex, we saw a man and a woman on the sidewalk: dressed only in a nightshirt and sneakers, she was taking off her shoes and throwing them into traffic as she walked away from the man, yelling. Realizing that drivers were wondering what was happening, she walked, barefoot, into the middle of the intersection and shouted: "Want to know what's happening? My boyfriend was sleeping around and I didn't know it and I got an STD!" Arms raised, she stood there, loudly proclaiming her misery to everyone within earshot and cursing herself for trusting this man. The lack of protection in her relationship—from a lack of public commitment to a lack of faithfulness, accountability, and support—had left her with no stability, no safety. Certainly, there was no blessedness in the scene. Most of the sexual revolution's relational catastrophes happen in private, but this very public revelation placarded the misery that Satan so likes to cover with a mask of freedom.

A Christian marriage brings safety in other physical ways, too. A recognition of the other person's standing before God—his or her personhood—is a guard. When we truly understand that our spouses are human beings made in God's image, we will be repulsed by anything that violates or demeans that standing. We will recognize and be disgusted by all sorts of abuse. To strike, demean, mock, sexually use, or do anything else that in any way ignores or belittles the image of God in this creature will be something that Christian spouses will not tolerate. And a marriage in which the spouses will not tolerate any kind of abuse from or in each other is a marriage in which personhood can safely flourish.

So often, we hear stories, or perhaps have experienced them, of marriages in which a spouse lived with violence and fear of physical harm. While it can stem from apparent relational unhappiness, violence certainly kills relational happiness. The necessity of physical safety in a one-flesh relationship is so fundamental that even our broken world recognizes it: domestic violence is still prosecuted as a crime, and perpetrators rightly carry heavy social stigma. Though men are statistically more prone to engaging in serious "intimate-partner violence," women increasingly are committing domestic abuse. Violence has no place in a true Christian marriage: believing spouses will not only reject abuse in principle but will also hate the thought of being abusive themselves. As someone who follows Jesus, the One who is gentle, meek, and lowly, incredibly patient with His bride and tender toward her, how could a believer think and act in any other way? Living in a marriage in which there is no fear of abuse, no threat of danger from a spouse, not even a worry of its possibility, is a safety that brings deep happiness.

This safety, of course, extends beyond the marriage itself. It is a happy thing to go through life knowing that your spouse will not allow you to be demeaned, mocked, or abused by those around you. Perhaps it is as quiet as a gentle rebuke to someone who has made your spouse seem lazy or irresponsible in a conversation. Maybe it is helping to end an unhealthy relationship with someone who is persistently damaging. Preserving a spouse's safety can be as dramatic as physically repelling an attacker, but it filters down to many little things in daily life.

A happy marriage also includes safety from gossip. It is the safety of earned trust, so that each spouse is secure in knowing that the other person protects you by refusing to discuss your weaknesses or struggles before others. Instead, a biblical marriage will be a place of finding help and safety in your spouse. It will be a refuge in a world where exposés and shaming are becoming routine and almost expected. It will be done not to ignore or hide sin but to "cover a multitude of sins" (James 5:20) from the eyes of people who have no business seeing it. "Faithfulness," John Milton noted, "is shown in the performance of promises, and the safe custody of secrets."[5] Being in a relationship in which your reputation is built up, your secrets are safe, and weaknesses and sins are covered by love to the fullest possible biblical extent means that you can be vulnerable, receive true help, and know that you will be built up, not torn down. That is blessing.

Safety in a happy marriage includes relational, not only physical and verbal, safety. A safe marriage is one in which there is no possible well-founded fear that a spouse is cultivating friendships that threaten the oneness of the marriage. The Billy Graham Rule—now often called the Mike Pence Rule—is something that our culture mocks. But people who follow it by refusing to be alone with a person of the opposite sex who is not their spouse, whether in a restaurant, office, car, or bed, give their marriages a sure safety. They have created safeguards not out of paranoia but out of a love for the spouse, building trust in their marriages. There is a happiness in the safety of a well-founded trust.

Marriage also gives us safety against loneliness. This was true before the fall: it was not good for Adam to be alone. That lack of goodness before sin was a lack of companionship and oneness. The dangers of loneliness are only greater now that we live in a fallen world. Loneliness is so prevalent in our culture that the U.S. surgeon general has issued serious warnings about it, noting that it can damage our health as much as smoking a pack a day.[6] Loneliness has major physical consequences. But the effects on our minds and souls may be even greater than the effects on our bodies. Loneliness opens us to depression, poor decision-making, poor personal care, and a willingness to befriend anyone, regardless of the person's true character and intent. In giving us marriage and the oneness that He designed to be part of it, God gives us protection against all these negatives—a protection that is the flip side of the joy of union.

Financial safety can feel like a relative thing, since riches, as Proverbs reminds us, can sprout wings and fly away (Prov. 23:5). So the safety that Christian marriage brings to finances is not a guarantee of economic prosperity.[7] It should, though, bring out the desire and wisdom to steward the money that God gives to best care for each other and together provide for those in greater need. Financial safety is a teaming up to use our resources for kingdom good, storing up treasures in heaven together. It is living with the knowledge that, being of the same mind, a spouse will not spend money foolishly or lavishly or make large purchases without discussion and mutual consent. This is true regardless of a couple's net worth: financial safety is a blessing that comes with faithfulness and oneness.

When a marriage has physical, financial, and relational safety, emotional safety will always follow. The relationship will be a place to confess hopes, dreams, fears, experiences—to have the vulnerability of honesty without fear. Having someone sympathize with weaknesses, quirks, or occasional silliness brings safety to a relationship and allows vulnerability to result in closeness, not distance. This does not mean that everything communicated to a spouse will have no consequences. Sometimes a confession of certain sin will bring effects that we still need to walk through. But in a safe marriage, it will be dealt with lovingly and even respecting our dignity. We see Joseph modeling this when he thought that Mary had been unfaithful to him. He could have been very public about this perceived breach of promise and relationship, but, being a righteous man, he "resolved to divorce her quietly" (Matt. 1:19). Emotional safety in a marriage brings joy and blessing even when there are issues that we need to deal with together.

Spiritual safety is not something that we tend to think about regularly—perhaps because we are less aware of the powers of darkness and spiritual forces of evil than we should be. Perhaps we think it is the responsibility of church leaders, not spouses. But as Christians who are the closest to each other, we can offer our spouses great spiritual safety. The Apostle Paul warns against people "without self-control" who "creep into households and capture weak women" (2 Tim. 3:3, 6). Being on the watch for "creeps"—false teachers with covert agendas, spiritual predators—helps spouses in another way to follow God's design for marriage as a safe place. This kind of watchfulness is safety from error: someone's speaking God's truth to you when you are tempted to the danger of unbelief and misbelief. This is true for husbands, since they bear the main responsibility for the spiritual safety of their families, but it is also true for wives, especially when they see or sense something disturbing first. Two sanctified heads are better than one.

But overt theological heresy is not the only spiritual danger. Trials, particularly long ones, open a marriage to discouragement and doubts. Christian marriage gives safety here as we remind each other of truths, of God's promises. Sometimes hardships are so deep and long that we become weary and broken down to the point at which we are unable to consistently speak the gospel to ourselves. In a Christian marriage, God has provided a spouse to do it. The happiness of having someone beside you providing perspective and encouragement, even through tears, is a precious thing. Ecclesiastes points out the blessing and safety inherent in this: "If they fall, one will lift up his fellow. But woe to him who is alone when he falls and has not another to lift him up!" (4:10). This is why the Westminster Confession of Faith identifies this kind of safety as a fundamental reason that God gave marriage to us: "for the mutual help of husband and wife" (34.2).

Such care for each other will create safety. And an attribute that inevitably accompanies safety in a happy marriage is calm: the trusting rest that comes from being quieted by real love. The multifaceted protection of a marriage that is in Christ gives not only the joy of safety but also the secondary happiness of peace. That does not mean that we will never be in a rush or have conflict or hurt feelings. It means that there is inner security through those things. It is a stillness and quietness that can exist because of safety—proven protection in a world that offers none.

The safety of a Christian marriage is a little picture of the safety of the believer's relationship with Jesus, not only individually, but also covenantally. It is protected and protecting because it is founded on the safety of the Lord's care for us. We experience this safety with spouses who are also in Christ as a good thing in itself, but it is also a foretaste of a promised fullness. At the end of time, when the Lord returns and puts everything right, God's sheep will "graze and lie down, and none shall make them afraid" (Zeph. 3:13). The threat of danger will not simply be limited or kept at bay; it will not exist. God's people will never again face any threat: "They shall dwell securely, and none shall make them afraid" (Ezek. 34:28). A happy marriage gives us a preview of this safety while we live on an unsafe earth. Outside circumstances might be dangerous and can even sometimes intrude into a relationship, but a marriage that is in Christ brings the joy of heavenly safety into a world that so badly needs it.

Story (1996)

After speaking on the phone for several weeks, John and Susan met in December 1994. At the time, John was in North Carolina and Susan was in Tennessee, and they had been introduced by a mutual friend. They were married in 1996 and now live in a large urban area in the United States.

Do you have a happy marriage?

Susan: We have a happy marriage if I define *happy* by "loving, committed, and reasonable." There have been and continue to be times when I don't like or appreciate the decisions that John makes. I grow impatient with his ways, and at times I don't respect the ways he parents our children. However, I always come back to the fact that God gave me John, who is a godly man and a strong leader. I truly believe that God saved him for me.

John: I am extremely happy to be married to Susan. The second day after I met her, I called her "dream girl," and I still tell her that is what she is to me. There are little things that Susan does that irritate me occasionally, but these things do not dull the affection and respect that I have for her.

How do you know that?

Susan: John overlooks my multitude of sins and annoyances. I feel relieved when I'm with him.

John: We enjoy each other's company.

What makes your marriage happy?

There are several things that we do together: being involved in the church, exercising hospitality, watching movies, going for walks and hikes, talking about the Bible and our future, praying together for each other and needs in our home and at church, and working on household projects. Also, Susan has a custom-home-decor business. We do installations together on Mondays and go to lunch together.

We have an emotional intimacy in that we can speak the truth to each other, regardless of how hard it is to say or to hear. We know each other's weaknesses and insecurities and try not to trample on them.

Each of us is convinced that the other is completely committed to the other. This makes for a security that is a prerequisite to happiness. We don't entertain other prospects.

John: I admire and respect Susan and have a debt of gratitude to her.

Susan: I admire and respect John, with an exception for some of the decisions he makes in parenting.

Has your marriage always been happy?

Susan: In the beginning, I was not happy and felt like I made a wrong decision to marry so soon after my divorce. My unhappiness was not entirely with John but with myself. I had been divorced for only two years when John and I started talking long-distance. I was attracted to him because he was a strong leader, was a man of God, and had lived the life he taught. He had been single for thirty-three years when we met. I knew that he had saved himself for marriage, which gave me great confidence that John would be faithful to me, unlike the marriage that I had come out of.

My unhappiness was due to the position that I put my two daughters in (eleven and twelve years old at the time). I moved them from Tennessee to North Carolina, to a new home, new church, new stepfather, new school, and new friends. The girls were troupers. They adjusted well to almost everything except a principled, deliberate, disciplined stepfather. I was often caught in the middle, softening tones, conversations, and instruction. Though they respected John, they did not like him. Once day, one of the girls came home from school early to see John eating lunch in the kitchen and said, "What's *he* doing here?"

After many struggles between John and the girls, we sought advice from another pastor, who had married a woman with children, who instructed me to be the main disciplinarian for a time (not the leader of the home, but enforcing discipline), and to allow the girls to see John as an ally and not an enemy. This worked. I set the rules and discipline, but I did so allowing the girls to see me conferring with John.

How did your marriage get to the place that it is now?

Over time, all four of us adjusted somewhat more to one another. Time was helpful.

What things have you found that detract from happiness in your marriage?

The biggest issue has been parenting two of our children who were/are extremely strong-willed. We had/have somewhat conflicting parenting styles. John is more rules-based and Susan is more grace-filled.

For many years, we lived under financial pressure. John felt pressure to live within our means. This often led to conflict at times when we could barely pay our bills.

How do you deal with remaining sin in yourselves in marriage?

We're both sickened by our sin, though we don't see it completely. We ask forgiveness for those offenses that we recognize that we've committed against the other. However, many of our sin patterns have tended to remain.

We call out to God in our personal prayers for Him to change our hearts. But we are slow to change.

What things have you noticed that drain happiness?

Susan: Having too many obligations (work, children, hospitality, church). When I feel that John expects too much of me when I already have a full platter, I become resentful.

John: When I feel that I am at the end of the line (behind kids, work, and others) and get what's left over.

Are there any habits or patterns that establish/perpetuate happiness?

Being faithful to each other: being a one-man woman and a

one-woman man. We should also have more relaxed alone time together, but we feel obligations to others.

Who are your marriage role models? Why?

There are several marriages that we admire from a distance, but we don't know any married couples well enough to be sure that we could look to them as role models.

Can you share one story or event that shaped/shifted your relationship or made you think differently about it or your spouse?

Susan: When we adopted our son, we were in our forties. It was a financial burden, but John knew it was the right thing to do. It made me see John not only as a frugal, disciplined man but now as one who would give of himself sacrificially.

How do you live with sadness in a good marriage?

John: Susan had ten miscarriages and one ectopic pregnancy. She also feels down at times due to stress, conflict, and guilt over past failures. I feel burdened for her and want her to know how much I care for her.

Susan: As far as my miscarriages go, I don't know how well I can describe the multiple losses. I learned from the first miscarriage that men and women handle miscarriage very differently. My first miscarriage was in 1998/99, one and a half years after a daughter was born. I was in the end of my first trimester when we discovered through a sonogram that our baby had no heartbeat. I was sad and confused and felt very empty. John seemed to take the news as a minor setback, but my mind was racing with thoughts about how I would never get to nurse this child or rock them to sleep or say bedtime prayers. . . .

I kept my emotions at bay because I didn't want to question God's plan for fear that I would somehow seem ungrateful for the children that He had already given me.

The other miscarriages took place between 2000 and 2004. They were all similar to the first miscarriage except for the second one. I had managed to get to twenty-one weeks. I was feeling movement and my body was showing signs of pregnancy. I was so thrilled, thinking that this pregnancy was going to last. I went in for my twenty-week sonogram and saw the heartbeat and learned that we were having our first son. The next day, I was not feeling movement. I called the doctor, and he said that I likely had not been feeling movement from the baby that was actually happening, but even if I hadn't, it was not unusual not to feel movement every day, especially so early. The next day, I asked to get a sonogram just to make sure that everything was OK. I got the sonogram and learned again that the baby had no heartbeat. The next morning, I went to the hospital to deliver our baby. When he was born, I saw his little formed body already at twenty-one weeks! His fingernails were already in place. His skin was translucent, but he was a little boy! I sobbed the rest of the day, and John was a great comfort. He shed a few tears and was obviously distressed but seemed to move on.

This miscarriage brought about a great sense of loss and uncertainty. Where was God? Didn't He know how much we desired a child, a son? The confusion was even more pronounced when my fifteen-year-old niece got pregnant in high school and carried to term.

I wasn't mad at God. I had seen through my Christian life that God is good, and I believed that He had plans to give me a hope and a future. After all, look at the gift that He gave me in John. Look at the three healthy children that I did have. At the risk of spiritualizing the situation, I have to say that I experienced great, supernatural hope. I couldn't understand how each time that I got pregnant, I had hopes and dreams for my child and never dwelled on the thought that this child would miscarry. After each miscarriage, I would say, "I just can't do this again." Yet amazingly, each time I got pregnant I was thrilled and excited and believed that this child would come to term. I think that kind of hope can come only from the Lord.

How have complicating factors shaped your marriage?

John: Susan was married previously to an unfaithful husband. So her default mindset has been to feel like damaged goods. This has also led Susan to resist giving herself emotionally to me. I adore Susan and have been trying to deprogram her emotions for many years.

Being a stepfather has been a complicating factor. My stepdaughters now look on me with appreciation and affection.

How do you "deprogram" someone's emotions—and what does it feel like to be deprogrammed?

Susan: Good question. What we mean by *deprogramming* is really *reframing* or speaking the truth to self. When I'm feeling shame or regret over my past, John will simply remind me who I am in Christ. He often tells me to preach the gospel to myself. Over nearly thirty years of marriage, he has spent a lot of time helping me put away old recordings of lies that I tell myself. Lies such as "I'm damaged goods," "I'm a hindrance to God's using John because he married a divorced woman," and "I wasn't strong enough spiritually to break the cycle of divorce." John reminds me that I am a new creature. Over the years, the truths of Scripture have almost negated the destructive ways of thinking.

I feel very grateful for John's taking his time to "deprogram" my harmful thinking. It's just a reminder of how much he cares for me and wants me to know and experience the love of Christ.

Scripture "deprograms" past failures, shame, and regrets by changing our thinking, which changes our behavior. The example that I always go back to is when Jesus is talking to the paralyzed man and sees him lying there. He says, "Wilt thou be made whole?" (John 5:6, KJV). I hear, "Do you *want* to get better?" I've learned to choose to *think* the truth whether I feel it or not. This has done the most to change my thinking.

What has your marriage been able to do because it is happy? What has been the fruit of your marriage outside of your happiness?

We are comfortable offering hospitality. We often have fun together and joke with each other. We've been an example to several people in the church, and we lead marriage classes there.

What encouragement would you give to someone in an unhappy marriage?

Stay married. Stay in prayer and find a trusted friend who will tell you the truth and always point you back to God's Word.

What is your favorite thing about being married?

John: Companionship.

Susan: Friendship.

7

Fruitfulness

Whoever abides in me and I in him, he it is that bears much fruit, for apart from me you can do nothing.
—John 15:5

Productivity is important in the twenty-first century, isn't it? Companies and individuals try to boost their productivity using methods, hacks, and incentives. There is a premium on productivity. Because we live in this culture, it is easy to confuse productivity with fruitfulness. But Scripture does not speak of productivity. It speaks of fruitfulness. Christians can be fruitful at any age, at any stage, and in any circumstances, because fruitfulness is a result of faithfulness. Note a fundamental difference between productivity and fruitfulness: you can have productivity without faith or real fruitfulness, but real faith will always lead to true fruitfulness, even without visible productivity. God, not culture, is the measure and grade of our fruitfulness because He is the One who enables our faithfulness and brings fruit out of it. He tells us that faithfulness is always fruitful—far more than mere productivity. And Christian marriages are designed to be places where fruitfulness flows out of faithfulness.

Just as fruitfulness is not productivity, so it is not giftedness. A very ordinary marriage between two average believers can be fruitful far beyond the relationship of "gifted" people. God does not value giftedness as much as He values loving faithfulness, and every Christian marriage has the opportunity to experience this joy. Because a Christian marriage is rooted in faithfulness—to God and each other—its fruitfulness has the joy of being freed from artificial and extrabiblical standards that we all tend to use when we measure fruitfulness.

Because the Lord promised that everyone who abides in Him will bear much fruit (John 15:5), we can expect that the union of two Christians will be fruitful. This is one significant reason to get married in the first place: two people realize that they are able to be and do more together, as a couple, than they would apart, as singles. The combination of particular gifts and strengths that would be more useful united than separate is a huge factor in choosing marriage with a particular person.

Fruitfulness in marriage is partly the product of peace. Christian marriage should be peaceful. This does not mean that there will never be a difference of opinion, serious questions back and forth, or iron sharpening iron—peace with error is not peace (Jer. 6:14)! That is because true peace can come only through true reconciliation and true safety—true love. A husband and wife who have each been reconciled to God through Christ's atonement are at peace with God, living according to the stability of His Word (Ps. 119:165). Secure in their relationship with Him, a Christian couple is able to be vulnerable, honest, and forgiving with each other, pursuing Christlikeness as a team. Sanctification for husband and wife is the inevitable result of a peaceful relationship. In Christ, marriage can be a place of true peace, and a marriage with true peace is a marriage worth fighting for.

Peace is freedom from conflict and oppression that results in fruitfulness. In a peaceful marriage, people can work, parent, create, fellowship, and worship. Those things are difficult or impossible when there is unchecked conflict, fear, or selfishness. A lack of fruitfulness reveals a lack of true peace just as much as conflict does. Real peace is the opposite of spiritual inactivity just as much as sinful activity is.

This is why peace does not equal space for video games, social media, or more "me" time. Aside from being generally unfruitful, these things tend to be unfulfilling and often eternally useless. Instead, in a Christian marriage, laziness, self-indulgence, and wrong priorities will die as true peace leads to fruitfulness. That does not mean that hobbies, vacations, and downtime are wrong. It means that they will be utilized as means to fruitfulness, not as ends in themselves or escapes from ordinary life callings.

The scenes connected with peace in the Bible are ones in which people are free from oppression and conflict and so are enabled to be incredibly fruitful. In a peaceful country, people can farm, get an education, use their creativity, serve their communities, worship, and more. People cannot do those things easily or at all when there is strife and oppression. In a peaceful home, people can play creatively, do homework, make supper, have useful conversations, read good books together, reach out to others, and more. People cannot do those things when there is strife and oppression. Biblical peace is neither inactivity nor mindless rest; it is happy service that is the fruit of harmony.

In 1 Corinthians, Paul explained that "God is not a God of

confusion but of peace" (1 Cor. 14:33). He was teaching the congregation at Corinth that their social chaos was stunting the church. Peace coming from love (ch. 13) would result in growth—in fruit. It was true corporately for the Ephesian church, it is true for nations through history, and it is true for a married couple. Relational peace creates a place where fruit will inevitably grow.

When there is a lack of relational peace, a couple's time, energy, and emotions drain into addressing the struggles and issues in the marriage. It is a drain on fruitfulness. But when a marriage in Christ is peaceful, husband and wife face life from a posture of support and fulfillment, allowing their time, energy, and emotions to be used to bless each other and those around them. God's love, when given to the Christian, not only will be an agent of internal personal change but also will overflow in fruitfulness, first to spouse and then from a couple to everyone around them.

This fruitfulness can take many forms, and it will be shaped by a couple's personalities, backgrounds, interests, health, wealth, and maturity. Within established patterns, God has given opportunity for great variety. Each Christian marriage will have its own thumbprint of fruitfulness as an externalization of each unique union. Specific expressions of fruit are some of the beautiful things to see in believing marriages around us.

But despite differences in situation and character, Christian marriages will share certain general aspects of fruitfulness, since they are the overflow of being in Christ together. Christian couples will be moving in the same direction toward the goal of glorifying God and loving those around them. Instead of pulling in many directions, true fruitfulness enables us to make advances in one direction, though it may manifest in different areas. For couples who are in Christ, the fruit of marriage may be varied, but it will all be pointing to the cross, facilitating their and others' glorifying God and enjoying Him forever (see Westminster Shorter Catechism 1). It will be Paul's "one thing I do" (Phil. 3:13) as he preached, wrote, mentored, traveled, prayed, and endured persecution, all as a means of "running the race" (see 1 Cor. 9:24). In this way, biblical fruitfulness is "the rational unification of the manifold."[1] And we can see it in the happiness of Christian marriage.

One happiness that is fundamental to fruitfulness is being in the Word and prayer together. When Jesus asked the Father in the High Priestly Prayer to "sanctify them in the truth," He also stated, "Your word is truth" (John 17:17). A couple's being in the Word together can take different expressions: a particular church, way of doing devotions together, and habit of family worship will each be a unique aspect of a Christian norm and will each bring blessing.

There is also happiness in coming together before the throne of grace. While prayer is certainly asking God for things that He has promised in His Word to give us, prayer is also fellowship. Some of the most fruitful people in the world are older saints who spend their time praying, physically unable to do anything else. While that is certainly not productive from an earthly perspective and is often unseen even by the church, it is something that bears incredible spiritual fruit—both in the person praying and in the people for whom he or she prays! Praying for each other in a marriage is a happiness in itself. When you look at your spouse and feel gratitude for him or her, you have the joy of thanking the Lord for the blessing of this relationship. Prayer for a spouse, especially over time, can bear abundant fruit as you see the Lord growing your spouse after the image of His Son. Prayer with each other enables you to better know and understand this other Christian and spiritually synchronize with him or her as you come before the Lord. It is fellowshipping with the Lord together, bringing the fruit of unity as well as the other blessings that God designed to go with prayer.

Opening a home to others is also a joy in Christian marriage. It takes two in a marriage to obey Scripture's hospitality commands (Rom. 12:13; 1 Peter 4:9), and couples who do also find blessing there. Despite the work involved, this biblical practice brings the fruit of working together, serving the saints, caring for strangers, and deepening fellowship. Even when hospitality leaves us disappointed or hurt because of sin, God can still use the fruit of our obedience. Some of the most hospitable people we know have been badly hurt by guests at some point. And just as often, we have seen that hardship bear fruit in closer marriages and families and greater reliance on the Lord to bring good out of any hospitable effort that we can make. As we use the resources of time, money, energy, and spaces that God gives to obey His call to hospitality, we will find that there is joy in this joint obedience.

A Christian marriage also has the joy of giving. Have you experienced the privilege of receiving more than you need and the fun of sitting down together to plan where to send it? The Lord has promised to reward giving that is not done for the admiration of other people (Matt. 6:1). Christian giving is an eternal investment, but it is already a blessing on this earth: a secret ministry that only the two spouses share as they invest money, often followed by prayer and love, that brings happiness as it blesses other believers or people in need. Giving also puts a couple's hearts in the same place as they store up treasure in heaven together (vv. 19–21).

But what about fruitfulness in the later years of a marriage?

Perhaps a mind or a body gives way, money dries up, children walk away from the faith, or energy becomes a precious commodity. For Christians, fruitfulness never ends. It can and does change shape, but it cannot and does not stop: "They still bear fruit in old age; they are ever full of sap and green, to declare that the LORD is upright; he is my rock, and there is no unrighteousness in him" (Ps. 92:14–15). Consistent use of the available means of grace continues to renew the inner man, even as the outer man wastes away (2 Cor. 4:16). Prayer and meditation on the Word are possible even when attendance in public worship is not, even when communication with a believing spouse is not. The Lord does not allow His people to not bear fruit (John 15:5).

There is also the fruit of faithfully caring for each other through sickness and aging. Our communities watch us—family, neighbors, and church. This witness of faithfulness can be an incredible testimony to other people, as God uses aging saints as examples and models as well as encouragements. Simply being faithful to each other "in sickness and in health," in strength and weakness, honors the Lord as He enables us to keep our vows and to demonstrate persistent love in difficult circumstances. This is wonderful fruit—perhaps the graduate school of a married relationship. If you have ever witnessed this in a happy marriage, you will have seen not only the increasing closeness of the couple but also the effect it has had on their children and congregation: something that often amounts to awe as the strong love of Jesus is lived out in weakness and pain. For unbelievers who watch, it is a gospel witness. For Christians seeing it, it bears the fruit of humility and gratitude.

One of the first Protestant marriages during the Reformation was Matthew and Katharina Zell's. Undertaken in defiance of Rome, illegal, and shocking, their union was not only happy, but also incredibly fruitful. This was their goal from the beginning. As a bride, Katharina wrote: "God grant that our marriage may thus endure, as it is now, until the end. So I hope it will, and may be pleasing to God and useful to both of our souls and advantageous in soul and body to many people."[2] The couple had two children; both died as toddlers. The faithful ministry that Matthew had was taken over after his early death by one of his students; this man dismissed Zell's example and began teaching heresy. Katharina had poured herself out in costly work in the congregation and community; this legacy was publicly discounted. There was no lasting productivity, nothing concrete left upon their deaths. But their marriage bore amazing fruit. Their courageous example of getting married was biblical inspiration for hundreds of other Protestants; their relationship to each other was deeply loving and enabled service to God's church that came from a love for Jesus; their legacy continues to encourage and instruct half a millennium later. Regardless of how productive, or even fruitful, we perceive our marriages to be, the Lord always uses faithfulness to bear fruit. When He enables us to be faithful, we can rest in the blessing of knowing that He will bring fruit out of it.

That is because real fruitfulness is an overflow of love: love for the Lord, brimming over in love for each other, and then spilling into family, church, and community. And though this sort of love will bear the most fruit within the couple, as they are sanctified, encouraged, and blessed, a marriage cannot contain it. The Lord has designed Christian marriages to be fountains that spill over. A fruitful marriage is one that brings blessing not only to the couple but also to all whom it touches. It may be physical expressions of love, it may be encouragement, it may simply be a silent example that is evidence of Jesus' love, but it will bear fruit. The marriage will be a producer, not a consumer. Increasingly freed from the poverty of its own problems—coming from narcissism, preoccupations, or even real needs such as unity—a healthy Christian marriage can extend God's love and peace to others as it becomes a conduit for blessing.

Story (1984)

On a Labor Day weekend in 1983, Nate arrived at Nicole's apartment to take her out on a blind date. Afterward, Nate followed through on a couple of dates with other women that he had already planned but has dated Nicole ever since. They were married at ages twenty-seven in 1984, and they currently live and work in a city in the northern United States. These answers are from both of them, but they come through Nicole's voice.

Do you have a happy marriage?

Yes! We enjoy being in each other's company and spending time together, doing life day-to-day or traveling and trying something new together. We laugh just about every day.

What makes your marriage happy?

The Lord is at the center of our marriage, and from that grows a desire to serve each other as we honor Him, through our commitment to Him and each other.

Has it always been happy?

No. Adjusting to marriage after we had both been single and independent for a number of years caused some tensions. Nicole also started a new job a month after our wedding, which was unexpectedly overwhelming, especially while also trying to be a perfect wife. Nate hit a wall his third year of medical school (which was our second year of marriage) and went through a period of depression, which we didn't really recognize at the time. In our third year of marriage, we welcomed our first baby, via unexpected C-section, and moved from Virginia to Maine ten days after the birth. Nate began his medical residency within the first few weeks, and for the first time in ten years, I was not working, living hundreds of miles from family, and learning that the people in Maine were very different from people in Virginia! Our "stress scores" were off the chart, yet we never considered that our marriage was at risk. The Lord was so gracious to lead us to a wonderful church (our intro to Reformed theology), a supportive Bible study for me, and an absolute dependence on the Lord.

You mention depression: how did that affect you both?

The depression was hard partly because we did not realize how bad it was at the time. During a particularly difficult surgery rotation, Nate came home one morning exhausted and sleep-deprived and said that he had looked at the doors of the hospital during the night and thought, "I could just walk out those doors and quit everything," and he almost did! Of course, that was a red flag, but he was so busy, we really didn't have time to talk about how he was feeling. I told him I was fine with his dropping out, but he had invested so much time and money that he needed to really think about it, talk to his adviser, and, of course, pray. He continued to persevere, and I prayed and tried my best to make our home a haven so that he could refuel when he was there. Our home became the study place for Nate and several other students, and I learned more about hospitality.

How did your marriage get to where it is now?

Work! We made the most of time we could spend together: dates, which became weekly after three children in four years; maintained a healthy sex life; and determined to grow together, not apart. We were blessed with a medical-school Bible study, which, despite the crazy schedules of four med students and four working wives, always found a weekly night to meet. We had great fellowship and accountability to God's Word and each other, which laid a foundation for making a church family a priority.

What things have you found that detract from happiness in your marriage?

Selfishness and busyness, work, and family (both our immediate and extended). We have asked how to use our God-given gifts to serve others while still making our marriage a priority and how to encourage each other to use our gifts or reframe, depending on the needs of each other and the family. We found that we had to extend much grace as we navigated determining God's will versus our own selfish desires.

How do you deal with remaining sin in yourselves in marriage?

Grace! We both realize that we will always battle our sin nature, especially selfishness, and need to extend grace to each other, as the Lord daily does for us. We know we will continue to be sanctified until we reach glory and will continue to need to say we are sorry when appropriate and be willing to forgive and forget.

What things have you noticed that drain happiness?

Financial stress, both good and bad—we hate tax time! Parenting differences—even with grown children, we still have to agree on decisions involving our time, money, and values as we navigate our relationships. We also have discussions regarding care for our elderly mothers and how we balance relationships with our siblings. We have faced some sad circumstances, but ultimately our faith in the Lord and each other has grown from each difficulty.

Can I ask what "good" financial stress is?

I was referring to situations where we have been blessed financially but did not agree completely on how to use the blessing. We are currently rethinking our will. We had to weigh investments, paying off debt, donations, and the fun purchase of a boat. There were days that we grew weary of discussions with financial advisers, figuring how conservative to be with investments, which charitable organizations vs. our church building project to donate to, and so on. For the first twenty years of our marriage, we had very little extra money to play around with, and as the years went on and more debt was paid off, we had to catch up on retirement investments and budget for college and weddings—all pretty clear decisions. To have "extra" money now is a blessing, but it can also be a challenge.

Are there any habits or patterns that help establish or perpetuate happiness for you?

Regular dates, even when the nest is empty—we still reserve most Friday nights for a date. Also being invested in our church together, serving together and encouraging each other in individual service. Regular church attendance, both Sunday school and worship services, as well as fellowship opportunities. We have been a part of a small group for more than twenty years, often hosted in our home and led by Nate, which requires planning and sacrifice, but which the Lord has always blessed more than we could imagine. We try to extend hospitality on a regular basis, both with our church family and with community friends. We also enjoy traveling together and learning to enjoy each other's interests. For example, Nate loves baseball, and over the years I have become a fan, as well as our kids. I am a huge beach lover, and Nate joyfully took me, and later our family, to the beach every year but one. We now own a beach house, which he enjoys almost as much as me!

Who are your marriage role models? Why?

We have been blessed with many strong marriages in our church and small group over the years. We benefited from excellent Sunday school classes on marriage and parenting where we got to know older couples and learn from their successes and failures, as well as form relationships that provided mentors for us to go to who knew us and our children. We also had role models that we did not want to emulate—mainly our parents. When we were first married, we discussed what aspects of our parents' marriages we did not want to imitate and worked hard to keep each other accountable when we saw each other fall into patterns from our childhood examples.

Can you share one story or event that shaped or shifted your relationship or made you think differently about it or your spouse?

When we moved to Maine a month before our third anniversary, we had no idea how difficult it would be to adjust to life in a strange state with very little support, a newborn, and so many demands on Nate—jumping right into a demanding medical residency (eighty-plus hours a week), a wife still recovering physically from a C-section, figuring out how to be a dad, and a whole house to set up and organize. But surprisingly, not only did we get it all together, but our memories are overall good! We realized that we were going to have to work as a team and just "do the next thing." Nate set up the entire kitchen, and I loved it! He had to trust me with the care of our child, often for a couple of days at a time without him at home. We grew in our trust in each other, and more importantly, we grew in our dependence on the Lord to provide wisdom, strength, and peace for very long days and nights.

How do you live with sadness in a good marriage?

Trust in God's providence and do not perseverate on our sadness, but instead remember our many blessings and how the Lord has sustained us in every difficult situation.

How have complicating factors shaped your marriage?

We haven't had any truly complicating factors, other than adjusting to Northern vs. Southern traditions and learning to live together after many years of being single. Having a sense of humor and frequently laughing about our differences made the transitions easier and usually fun.

Our oldest child and only son is a prodigal, and that has been heartbreaking and stressful. We have had to juggle emotions and practical matters regarding that (live-in girlfriend, rejecting his faith, etc.) and swallow our pride as we ask for prayer and wise counsel from our church family. Our main prayer, besides the return of our son to the Lord, has been for us to see what the Lord is teaching us about ourselves and our relationship with each other and Him.

What has your marriage been able to do because it is happy? What has been the fruit of your marriage outside of your happiness?

Because our marriage is happy, we've had many opportunities to mentor and serve young couples and couples struggling in their marriages. Two of our three children are married, and we feel that we set a good example (not perfect by any means!) for how they should approach the institution of marriage. So far, they both seem to have very happy marriages. We also pray that we are encouraging our grandchildren to have strong marriages by our example.

Since we are content and secure in our relationship, we have more energy to invest in our church family and support each other in using our gifts as much as possible. We also know each other well enough to know when it's appropriate to say "no" to opportunities that are good, but would overextend us.

What encouragement would you give to someone in an unhappy marriage?

Seek counseling if you have not done so. If you are Christians, we encourage you to continue to pray for each other, read God's Word, and talk through your problems. We also remind you that you can change only yourself and how you react to problems. You cannot change another person; only the Lord can do that.

What is your favorite thing about being married?

Comfortable companionship—the security of always having your best friend to go through life by your side.

8

Community

And let us consider how to stir up one another
to love and good works, not neglecting to meet together,
as is the habit of some, but encouraging one another,
and all the more as you see the Day drawing near.
—Hebrews 10:24–25

No marriage exists in true isolation. It is not possible, since interaction with others is necessary for a functional life, even if it is only speaking to the dentist and the children's teacher. But when there is not healthy community, there is danger. If a couple are not part of a solid community, they are either selfish or in trouble—or both. Proverbs warns us, "Whoever isolates himself seeks his own desire; he breaks out against all sound judgment" (18:1). It is not only difficult but also unhealthy to live in isolation. A couple who refuse fellowship are raising a huge red flag. The opposite is true, too, though: God gave us community partly to bring happiness to our marriages. Fellowship is a tool for spiritual growth. It is a gift that is there for the taking. Like so many other design elements that God gave for our joy, community is a multifaceted blessing to Christian marriage.

A wedding itself is embedded in community: family and church view a public covenant ceremony, not only sharing the couple's joy but also functioning as witnesses. Perhaps you have attended a wedding at which the pastor asked, "If anyone here present knows of any cause why these two may not be lawfully joined, let him now declare it, or forever hold his peace." The community's knowledge of the bride and groom's pasts is a resource that confirms or denies the legitimacy of the marriage. Thankfully, it is rare for someone to speak up in response to this challenge! The silent, communal affirmation that this union is legitimate is a blessing.

The congregation at a wedding is also a silent witness to the couple's vows. Dozens or hundreds of people saw and heard the exchange of rings and promises to be faithful "till death do us part." There is a reason behind this. Not only are the spouses accountable to each other in marriage, but their marriage is also accountable to a biblically shaped community if they are Christians. And this is not a burden but a blessing. To know that you or your spouse will be called back to better loving and cherishing by someone who witnessed your promises is a necessary safeguard. The community at a wedding functions as an aspect of security for our marriages that we can depend on if things get rough.

But the community is also there to celebrate—to delight in the formation and growth of a new covenant family. Accountability and support go hand in hand with joy. The community's confirmation and celebration of a couple's committing to each other is a joy that carries into the future as the community continues to support and celebrate the life of a biblical marriage.

When a couple comes back from their honeymoon, the journey of integrating into a community as husband and wife—instead of singles—begins. They might not be consciously thinking of this; "leaving and cleaving" and the fun of establishing their own household might be first on their minds. They may still be in honeymoon mode, content to sit and gaze into each other's eyes. But as Martin Bucer pointed out, "Leaving a father and mother, therefore, does not mean that 'the married partners now no longer love their parents and all their in-laws, because they are completely absorbed in each other; on the contrary, marriage now enables them to love all those others more cordially and perfectly than they did before.'"[3] From the security of a loving relationship, a couple can better focus on serving those around them. The significant and time-consuming process of finding a spouse is done; the couple can move forward together. As they do so within the context of the church community, they are able to enjoy the blessings that God designed to go with that position.

In giving Christian marriage the blessing of a church community, God gave couples a living, breathing library of examples and role models. Everybody's ideas about marriage are initially shaped by parents, for better or for worse. Sadly, the context of contemporary culture compounded by personal sin means that a lot of people, including Christians, have grown up without a solid, biblical model of happy marriage. In doing premarital counseling, my husband and I have increasingly found that young, believing couples are hungry for healthy examples outside their families because brokenness in their parents' relationships has left large relational questions for them. By providing a congregation around a couple, God gives the blessing of seeing a wide variety of backgrounds, personalities, and life stages expressed in unique marriages. This is not simply to expand a couple's knowledge of what works but to allow them to see what is possible, beyond what one set of parents could show them, even if that example was healthy. The principles of a Christian relationship are practiced in many variations in a Christian community. Individual couples live out presuppositions in ways that they are able. Older and godlier marriages can give younger couples incredible blessing as they live out wisdom and freedom within biblical bounds. Community allows us to see pictures of Christ and His church functioning in sickness and health, poverty and wealth, for better or for worse.

This is very much tied to balance in marriage. Just like an individual, a relationship can be turned in on itself. A church community, with all its variety, helps keep a relationship in healthy proportions. Without external examples and supports, a relationship can become too idiosyncratic for fruitfulness. Hobbyhorses and personal interests can facilitate self-obsession; a healthy community will always, simply by its existence, be calling us out of that as we hear of needs, see different situations and people, and are stretched outside our comfort zones by them. Our marriages receive the gift of increasing well-roundedness in a Christian fellowship.

But a community is more than a collection of role models; it is a resource of wisdom. We can go to other older, more experienced couples around us for more than example. This is true for practical, everyday things: there is almost always someone in a congregation who can give you the name of a good roofer or babysitter or answer questions about starting a garden. Maybe we need counsel for preventive measures: how did a happy older couple navigate family issues together during the holidays? What are the best tips for doing family road trips? But a community is there for the harder questions, too. If you are in a gospel-believing congregation, other couples have navigated every trial common to marriage. We can go to discreet couples and ask about dealing with conflict, disagreements in parenting choices, tensions over finances, coping with disappointments in each other, facing loss and grief united, and much more. A community will enable us to take biblical principles of marriage and help us practice them in our unique situation. In a multitude of counselors there is safety (Prov. 11:14), and God gives our marriages this gift in the context of fellowship.

The blessings of examples and wisdom give our marriages the added blessing of encouragement. There are few things more heartening for a relationship than seeing older relationships that are healthy, strong, and happy. This is true for marriages that are struggling: when we look around at older couples who have weathered decades together and are somehow still happy, we know that there must be hope for our own marriages. The couples in your congregation—especially the older ones—have survived more storms than newlyweds can imagine. They have been able to do so by God's grace working in their lives in ways that young saints have yet to experience. If Jesus taught and preserved them, He can also preserve younger, weaker relationships. But the encouragement of an older, strong marriage is not only for couples who are dealing with discouragement in each other; it is also for other happy marriages. Seeing another couple enjoy the same blessings that you do can create a bond as well as appreciation for the good gifts that God loves to give His children—a rejoicing with those who rejoice. And whether your marriage is struggling or strong, seeing a couple love each other year after year, through different seasons, challenges, and valleys, is encouraging as we see the perseverance of the saints in this particular aspect of the pilgrim journey. It certainly makes a community a stronger, happier place to be.

We also receive the gift of a broader safety in a healthy community. One elderly retired pastor used to come up to me once in a while and ask, “Is this young man treating you well?” He certainly was. “If that ever changes, let me know!” Though I never needed protection, this older Christian and his wife gave the open offer of safety for my marriage. They were there for the marriages around them, watching out for the health and happiness of younger relationships. We need people like this: not only those whose discretion we can count on and whose judgment we can trust when we go to them, but people who will come to us when they can see that something is not right. Maybe it is an older woman seeing the distance created by a fight on the way to church and asking whether you need a hand with the children so that the two of you can talk; perhaps something serious is going on and a church needs to provide protection. A woman whose marriage was initially struggling told me much later that despite physical distance in a pew, emotional distance during social times, and an unhappy countenance, nobody in her large congregation asked whether everything was all right or got to know the young couple well enough to find out. A healthy community will be watching out for each other’s marriages and will have the relational connection and tools to bolster safety. Big or little, a church community is there to provide protection for a marriage, but also for the individuals within the relationship.

A healthy church will care for a marriage in happy times, such as the arrival of a baby, providing meals, onesies, and encouragement. We have seen dozens of international seminary students enabled to welcome little ones in a foreign country when they had no money, family, or knowledge of a medical system, simply because of the love of a congregation. The church community will also be there in hard times: long or serious illnesses, griefs, hardships such as unemployment, family division, and more. In one congregation that we were part of, an elderly man and his adult children needed additional people to sit with his terminally ill wife as he arranged hospice care; the church provided a constant stream of fellow believers who went in shifts for days to be with her, enabling her husband to provide care for her final days without burning out. Congregations are there to rally around a couple with meals and encouragement but also counsel, financial support, and the love of Jesus' body.

A great gift that a church community gives a marriage is prayer. Learning how to pray with each other is certainly included here, but an equally great and often unseen blessing is having others pray for you in your marriage. Perhaps the older woman will tell you that she is praying for you; perhaps she will do it silently for years. Pastors and elders often intercede for the marriages in the flock, from the pulpit and in a closed study. All these petitions for us go up to the Lord and He answers them, whether or not we are aware of the answers. Regardless of our own awareness, these are gifts from the Lord that He uses to bless us, even when we are oblivious. One of the joys of heaven will be seeing and understanding all the prayers from fellow saints for our marriages.

But being part of a community goes both ways: it will pour into us, and we can pour into it. Part of the joy of being part of a community is the happiness of investing in it as a team. Maybe it is bringing meals to people who need them, caring for extended family, going on mission trips, or volunteering at a local soup kitchen or shelter. One couple we know took a leap and volunteered to teach the three-year-old Sunday school class together—and ended up loving it, together forging relationships with some of the youngest people in the congregation. Another was always on call to invite church visitors over for a meal. Some worked as a team behind the scenes to care for shut-ins. A happy marriage is one that will bear fruit, and community gives a beautiful outlet for a couple to use their gifts together to build up the body of Christ. It is a place to cast bread upon waters, to sow seed, to lay up treasure in heaven. The immediate and long-term—actually eternal!—blessings that come with this bring joy to a couple. Sinclair Ferguson points out that when we use our gifts to serve, the "result, both individually and corporately, is our growth in maturity (Eph 4:12–16)."[4] Fruitful service actually enriches a marriage.

Perhaps, though, the most significant reason that God put our marriages in community is what we see in other Christian marriages. While they do give us role models to follow, wisdom, blessing, safety, and prayer, there is actually a bigger reason for having access to other believers' relationships. Marriage is to be a picture of Christ and His church. But one human example can never span or portray the complete fullness of the Real. Having many marriages around us, each with a different history, culture, and function, not only gives us examples and balance; it actually enables us to better understand the relationship of Christ and the church. In different marriages, we see different expressions of love, varied examples of sacrifice, many kinds of service and submission. We see more facets of Christ's love for His bride than one finite relationship can show. Community is not just for our marriages but for our spiritual health as Christians also as we gain a broader and deeper understanding of what Jesus' love is and means. That will certainly shape our marriages as that knowledge percolates through our minds and hearts into our relationships.

A marriage that is grounded in a Christian community will be a marriage that is cultivated and cared for from the outside. It will have the blessings of support and help. A Christian community gives us pictures that we cannot see on our own. Through this design, God gives Christian marriages stability and support throughout a relationship—and then stability and support for the spouse who outlives the marriage. The happiness of community is there for a Christian marriage, from start to finish.

Story (1978)

Mike and Andrea are from the Midwest. They were married in 1978, have multiple children, and enjoy an ever-increasing array of grandchildren.

How did you meet?

Andrea: Mike and I met at church. He was a college student. I was a new convert. We were both attending the same church. We met in August 1976. The college group from church organized a canoe trip. I was in a canoe with another guy, he with another girl. We were all just friends. The canoe I was riding in tipped over, and I didn't have the strength to help put the canoe upright. All of the group just canoed on by us as we were walking in the river. Mike was the only one to stop, jump out, and help get the canoe turned over and get us back in. On the way home, Mike sat down next to me on the bus, and as any gentleman would, he held my wet socks.

Do you have a happy marriage?

Yes. We like each other. We enjoy talking together, working around the house together, going places together. We are still married after forty-five years! Still committed to each other, still friends.

What makes your marriage happy?

Andrea: We try to put the other first, to help each other. We are opposites in how we like to spend our free time, but we make a point to spend time together doing what the other enjoys.

Mike: Being content with what you have is important. Not to have an unrealistic view of the perfect marriage (it doesn't exist) and trying to achieve it. Andrea and I have the same worldview: how the world works and how we want to live in it. This comes from our shared faith in our sovereign God, and knowing that His Son is our personal Savior.

Has your marriage always been happy?

Andrea: It's always been pretty happy. We've had seasons of animosity toward the other. The Lord has used church, friends, and His Word to show me where I have been mean, selfish, and stubborn. He has helped me to go to Mike and ask for forgiveness. The Holy Spirit has prompted me and given me the strength to make changes.

Mike: A happy marriage is not the goal. It is the journey both of you are on. Our marriage has its ups and downs. A happy marriage is not about avoiding hard times; it is being able to respond correctly to adversity. Marriage is a lot of hard work. We have learned that responding correctly to circumstances influences our happiness more than the events themselves do.

How did your marriage get to where it is now?

Andrea: We have been faithful to and patient with each other. There is a strong bond that we have together.

Mike: Both of us are growing in our walk with the Lord. We take difficult things to Him in prayer. We try to keep talking and work out the problems. We are willing to forgive and not carry grudges. I try to concentrate on Andrea's positive aspects.

What things have you found that detract from the happiness in your marriage?

Andrea: I can concentrate on Mike's shortcomings to where I can be upset with him over the smallest things. These small things get bigger to me, and I find I am very intolerant and not fun to be around.

Mike: When we try to change the other person. We are guilty of doing too many good things instead of setting aside time for each other.

How do you deal with remaining sin in yourselves in a marriage?

When convicted, we usually need time alone to pray. This time helps us reflect on our own sin. We try to listen to God's voice. We're a couple who, with God's help, ask each other for forgiveness. It's not always easy to forgive and forget. The longer we have been married, we have gotten better at this. It is very important to uphold each other in prayer.

What things have you noticed drain happiness?

Andrea: Discontentment. Focusing on the other's weakness. I find that my reactions can be more intense; I'm more easily upset at Mike for the littlest things.

Mike: Selfishness. Using words that wound your partner. Anger. Having unresolved conflicts.

Are there any habits or patterns that establish and perpetuate happiness?

Sharing responsibilities: Mike has started emptying the dishwasher and Andrea on occasion waters flowers or weeds the garden. Being a good listener. Staying in the Word.

Who are your marriage role models?

An elder and his wife. They are really supportive to each other and committed to their Lord and Savior.

Also a pastor and his wife. They truly put the other first; they are very selfless, godly people. We admire how they brought the Word to their children; their family was centered on the Word.

Can you share one story or event that shifted your relationship or made you think differently about your spouse?

Mike: I'll never forget how Andrea cared for her mother in her last days. Andrea was willing to give up her time to be there. I saw in Andrea another level of self-sacrifice that I hadn't before.

Andrea: I've seen a change in Mike over the years. He has truly shown Christ to me as we live our daily lives. I've brought a lot of baggage to our marriage, being from a divorced family and having a difficult relationship with my mother. I have not been easy to live with, yet Mike has been very loving and self-sacrificing. His love turns me to my Savior as I see His love lived out every day.

How do you live with sadness in a good marriage?

Andrea: When we had a miscarriage, we didn't push the other person away. We grieved together, prayed together. In the midst of great sorrow, the Lord brought us closer.

How have complicating factors shaped your marriage?

Andrea was a city girl and Mike was a country boy. We had to compromise. Not all of our vacations were in the wilderness, nor were there days at the shopping mall. Andrea goes canoeing and Mike takes ballroom dancing lessons.

What has your marriage been able to do because it is happy?

We have been able to serve the church in many ways. We support one another and are able to give the other freedom to serve in their own way.

The biggest fruits are seven children who are adults now, raising children of their own. They are all serving their families and their churches in different ways. We thank the Lord that He has graciously saved each one of our children and is using them in His kingdom!

What encouragement would you give to someone in an unhappy marriage?

Andrea: I truly believe that there is always hope, that your marriage can be better. I would encourage them to seek a godly counselor. But I also realize that it takes two to want to make it better. Being in an unhappy marriage would be one of the most difficult things to live through. I would point them to the Lord and encourage them to see Him, trust Him, because that is the only way to survive great unhappiness in life.

What is your favorite thing about being married?

Andrea: I love having someone to share my ordinary life with. Someone I can tell all my troubles, someone who loves me in spite of my shortcomings. Mike is a great sounding board. He is good at helping me be a better person.

Mike: Having a safe place to come together to get away from the cares of the world. Eating dinner on the patio together. Sharing the little things, like watching Halley's Comet in the middle of a cornfield.

9

Worship

Now [He] is able to strengthen you
according to my gospel and the preaching of Jesus Christ, . . .
to bring about the obedience of faith.
—Romans 16:25–26

Public worship is perhaps the most underestimated blessing for a marriage. It does not seem obviously connected to a husband-wife relationship, especially at a time in history when church often looks more like consumerism than worship. And certainly, the chief end of worship is not stronger marriages. But in a healthy church, stronger marriages are one inevitable result of worship that glorifies God. Within the context of a biblical local church, under a living pulpit ministry, a couple can really experience the happiness in a marriage that is a symptom—a joyful byproduct—of public worship.

That is precisely because true worship is not about us: it is about God. It reorients us to a heavenly-mindedness. It gives us perspective. And if worship is part of God's design for humanity in general, then it is certainly going to affect each marriage that takes it seriously. In his book *Knowing God*, J.I. Packer describes the Christian life as running on worship. If that is true for the individual, it is true for the life of two believers in covenant. Marriage runs on worship, because worship points us to eternal worship and places our marriages in spiritual and temporal perspective. It is a regular, reliable reorientation to what Elisabeth Elliot called "the straightedge of Scripture."[1] The Lord gives us the Lord's Day as a joyful command that is for our happiness: "Above all you shall keep my Sabbaths . . . , that you may know that I, the LORD, sanctify you" (Ex. 31:13). After all, the will of God is our sanctification (1 Thess. 4:3); a marriage that knowingly rejects this knowingly rejects blessing.

Worship is the public assembly of God's people to praise Him in song, prayer, and offerings; to learn His will from His Word; and to receive the sacraments of baptism and the Lord's Supper at appropriate times as means of grace. The preaching of the Word is of particular importance, since the Bible teaches that it is the most usual way that God converts unbelievers and sanctifies believers. Public worship allows the Christian soul to "adorn [itself] with gladness" in Christ: "Jesus, source of lasting pleasure, / truest Friend and dearest treasure, / peace beyond all understanding, / joy into all life expanding."[2]

Christian marriage actually begins with public worship: the wedding service, with prayers, Scripture reading and teaching, and congregational singing, in addition to the vows and other wedding elements. Beginning a marriage with this sort of worship is unique to Christianity. If you watched the two Jordanian royal weddings in 2023, you will have noticed something interesting. These visually stunning ceremonies, full of flowers and architecture and pomp, had no music, no congregational singing, not even an open Qur'an. Despite some thoughts from an imam, these events were not worship services but civil ceremonies. Hindu weddings are much more religious, making offerings to try to gain a god or goddess's blessing, but they are very much concerned with the family alliance and appropriate social arrangements. There is no corporate worship as thanksgiving. Attend a secular Western wedding, and it is entirely horizontal, with humanist vows, music that has no grounding outside personal taste, and all admiration directed to the couple and their mutual affection. If you have had the joy of worshiping at a Christian wedding, you know the difference. It is not ultimately about the couple, though their wedding is an opportunity to thank God for His particular kindness to them. A Christian wedding celebrates God's goodness to His creation and His people, the couple as well as the community and family that surround them. Such a wedding is redeemed and different. So worship shapes a Christian marriage from the very start, but it is only the beginning of how it brings happiness to a relationship.

Worship keeps us from becoming self-oriented. Every marriage needs this, even (and perhaps especially) ones that are generally happy, with no obvious issues. Those are the marriages most prone to coasting. If there is nothing obviously broken, we often think that there is nothing to fix. Worship keeps those marriages from becoming relationally narcissistic, revealing ways that God calls us to sanctification even in joyful relationships. Worship ministers as much to happy marriages as it does to marriages that are hurting and in clear need of help.

Worship also allows us to offer thanksgiving for God's good gifts, including marriage. C.S. Lewis pointed out that one of the tragedies of unbelief is that when thanksgiving wells up, there is nowhere for it to go. Worship allows us to praise God for who He is, what He has done, and the gifts that He has given. Thanksgiving is actually a blessing for Christian marriage that is another aid in directing our gaze heavenward.

When our marriages do make use of worship, they are embedded in a context that actually spans time and eternity. We are joining in the corporate praise of heaven, with angels and saints triumphant. Our most important, though temporary, relationship is placed within the context of our eternal relationship with the triune God. Eternity, not marriage, is the ultimate end. Worship puts marriage in its temporal place.

As we leave our "worldly employments and recreations" (Westminster Shorter Catechism 60) aside on the first day of each week and gather with the people of God, we state that our interests, our agendas, and our schedules are not our top priorities. Few of us would ever say verbally that life is about us, but we often live as though it is. The most useful thing to any marriage—struggling or not—is not a book on marriage. It is worship. It is submitting publicly and side by side to the Lord's Word and will for our lives.

Worship is also a leveler. Each person present is a creature before a Creator; a sinner before a holy God; a Christian beloved by the Father, redeemed by the Son, and sustained by the Holy Spirit. Where is boasting? Pride has no place before the cross. This equalizing effect of worship is true socially in a broad way: in one congregation where my husband and I worshiped, there was a member of the House of Lords sharing a songbook with a man with Down syndrome. If worship can flatten the greatest social barriers, it can also destroy barriers that we put up in marriage. Earthly comparisons collapse as we see again the greatness of our Creator and Savior. Worship is the great equalizer, in which husband and wife are free to worship the same Trinity together, with no rank or position or imagined status coming between them.

Worship is the great humbler. When we come before the Lord together and praise Him for who He is, for mercy that we do not deserve—if we actually understand that—annoyances and pet peeves and petty bickering will be shown for what they are. The little kingdoms that we build in marriage and in life dissolve as we are confronted by the kingdom of our God and of His Christ. The real King's glory pushes back our own ideas of or inclinations to self-supremacy. Our grasping for supremacy dies and the blessings of humility and contentment can flourish in a worshiping marriage.

Worship is also a clarifier. We all have our own way of seeing things, and to the extent that we are blinded by sin and distorted by experience, we all filter our vision through self and fallen reason. So spouses often function with discrepancies in their vision, which can bring disunity to a relationship. Sinclair Ferguson observes: "None of us sees clearly. We constantly misinterpret reality. . . . Only in God's light do we see light (Psa. 36:9). We come into his presence, we bow 'before Jehovah's awful throne,' and stability returns."[3] Having our vision cleared as we say, "Amen," and turn to our spouses has huge ramifications for marriage. It means that we will look at our marriages more and more as they really are, not as we have been assuming they are. We will start to see our marriages less from our own distorted perspective and more from God's as worship corrects our spiritual sight. This is the joy of seeing things from the same biblical perspective.

The same worship that brings clarity also provides help. When we see things as they are—when we see ourselves as we are!—we also see our needs. The same grace that offers sight offers cleansing. Part of the joy of worship is, together as a couple, seeing our sins, repenting of them, and taking hold together of the cleanness and fresh start that God offers to His children through Jesus. It is the happiness of being told again, "Behold, . . . your guilt is taken away, and your sin atoned for" (Isa. 6:7). It is the joy of a marriage freed from the guilt and power of sin.

Worship is a maturing thing. Our world is immature and happy about it. At least, it is happy in the moment. Immaturity may seem like fun in the short term, when it looks like staying up too late and binge-watching movies or splurging with money that we do not have. Immaturity never brings blessing, though. And despite our culture's suppression of maturity, very few people want to marry an immature spouse. We know that maturity provides stability and happiness in the long term. Loving worship, being in worship together, is a mark of maturity to start with: "Maturity, [Paul] contended, was not to be measured by [the Corinthians'] gifts but by their desire for the presence and power of God."[4] We can see what real maturity is in our Lord and the blessing it brought to those around Him, especially those closest to Him. Worship is not only a catalyst for maturation but also the place where we see and come to know true maturity. Jesus is the incarnation of maturity, and seeing Him in worship gives us categories that we do not naturally have. It gives us the desire to follow Christ in this but also the power of the Spirit to grow in maturation.

Biblical, balanced preaching also brings happiness to a marriage. That may sound odd—why would preaching play an important role in a marriage? Whatever problems a relationship has had in the past week, coming together, bowing in corporate worship, and hearing

God speak to His people through a faithful pulpit ministry will bring help to a marriage. It does not simply give perspective and new categories of thought, though it certainly will if it is faithful to the Word. Because preaching communicates to us God's will, because it is actually the Lord speaking through one of His servants, preaching addresses issues and places that other things cannot. When the Spirit applies the Word, we are enabled to love and forgive and grow in ways that we did not even know we needed.

I come from a family of pastors (three by blood, four by marriage); they could fill a whole book with stories of how Spirit-blessed preaching has changed marriages in their congregations. When Christ speaks to His people through preaching, there is direct, often intense counseling happening right there in the pew, in public. It may be addressing a personal issue that has been crippling a marriage. It may be directly dealing with a relational problem, public or private. As the Spirit applies the preached Word to the souls and minds of believers, the Word addresses issues that other means do not, simply because it has a power that other means do not. It even gets to issues that we did not know we had—perhaps that our spouses are also unaware of. Sins and weaknesses that we were ignorant of before the law came come to light through the preached Word (Rom. 7:7). Preaching does not necessarily tell us how to have happy marriages, but through the Spirit, it has the power to make us the kind of people whose marriages will be happy in Jesus. That is God's sanctifying grace to us in our marriages.

Grace, one of my pastors says, is not always comfortable because it is concerned about our character more than our comfort. But the Word declared does not only expose the sins and weaknesses that beset us; it actually has the power to deal with them. Perhaps we know that there is an issue that needs to be dealt with, but we feel helpless. Perhaps we were blind to something, and we need the Word to bring awareness (Rom. 7:7). When the Spirit accompanies the preached Word, we can expect holiness and joy to follow. Preaching gives the joy of being sanctified by the Word and seeing its effect in each other. Attention to the Lord's Word and commandments brings peace and even blessing to children (Isa. 48:18–19). It can actually clean us up individually and clean up our marriages, bringing growing peace between spouses even as it brings growing peace between saved sinners and God. "Sanctify them in the truth; your word is truth" (John 17:17). Preaching, Charles Spurgeon told his students, is "the inspiring of saints to nobler things, the leading of Christians closer to the Master."[5] For Christians, this closeness is joy.

Part of this closeness to God through preaching comes from repentance and faith. Ferguson explains: "When we hear the word of God expounded in the grace and power of the Holy Spirit, we are listening to the voice of the Good Shepherd himself. . . . He has promised to illumine and renew our thinking, to expose our sin so that we may see, feel, and confess it, and experience its forgiveness. It is through preaching that Christ will heal our hurts and strengthen us to live for the glory of God."[6] Is there a marriage in the world so happy that this kind of experience cannot deepen its joy?

Preaching also gives the joy of hearing again together of God's love for His people. We need this, don't we? The world is often an unhappy place, and discouragement can be not only around us, but also in us as we go through the daily grind, battling sin, schedules, sickness, and other fallenness. The good news that God so loved the world, that He has our names written on His hands, that He carries lambs and leads sheep, that His yoke is easy and His burden is light—these are truths that preaching provides anew every week. It reminds us of God's love for us, and fuels our love for each other. A marriage running on God's eternal love will have joy for life in a fallen world.

Worship also shows us what real love looks like. The Lord's Supper is a physical reminder of the Father's love in Christ that we get to remember with the rest of God's children.[7] If we are believers, beholding this love will inevitably change us. When we see Him in person, we will be made like Him. In a small way, the same thing happens in worship, maybe particularly in the context of communion: "Never to my hurt invited, / Be Thy love with love requited; / From this banquet let me measure, / Lord, how vast and deep its treasure."[8] The reminder of real love is essential to happiness in a marriage. Beholding love that moved in a way that we have not and cannot is something that humbles us but, in union with Christ, gives us true access to that kind of love, both as we receive it and as we seek to show it to others.

"See what kind of love the Father has given to us," John wrote, "that we should be called children of God; and so we are" (1 John 3:1). For married Christians, being fed with the same food by the same Father emphasizes the primacy of our relationship with Him, but also our fundamental relationship of spiritual siblings to our spouses. This is the aspect of our relationship that will outlast time, and it facilitates our joint knowing God and enjoying Him forever: as we understand Christ's love for the church, it will help us better care for and enjoy each other (Eph. 5:25–27). It is the joy of jointly feeding on Christ, who has become our "righteousness and sanctification and redemption" (1 Cor. 1:30). This true love cannot but bring blessing to a marriage.

And worship gives direction to a marriage. It brings meaning by reminding us of the joy of the hope of the glory that awaits. Regardless of whether our marriages are currently blissful or struggling, the joy set before us gives us happiness in knowing that this is not the end and that our Father will bring us safely home.[9] Life in even the happiest marriage is far less happy than life in glory. This knowledge can fuel happiness between husband and wife as they sharpen their understanding of it and run toward it together.

But there is a very practical side to the direction as well. When our lives are rightly centered on the worship of God, priorities fall into place, including relational priorities, schedules, and financial commitments. So do our own desires and ambitions. As we worship a God whose character and being are marked by simplicity, we become less complicated ourselves. Life can be messy because we are messy. Robert Frost described it as having his arms too full of packages: "For every parcel I stoop down to seize, / I lose some other off my arms and knees, / And the whole pile is slipping . . . , / Extremes too hard to comprehend at once."[10] We can forget our God-given limitations and callings as we accumulate more goals, priorities, choices, connections, appointments, and stuff than our finitude allows. Worship realigns us, bringing us back to the "one thing" that is essential (Ps. 27:4; Luke 10:42; Phil. 3:13). As couples come together before the throne, we gain focus, becoming less scattered. We may still have full schedules and things to sort through, but life will become more unified—directed to beholding the Lord's face and pressing on toward the goal. For a marriage, this straightening out clarifies a lot. Christian husbands and wives who are shaped by worship will be more single-minded and in agreement, less stretched between competing influences and goals.

Worship gives us the happiness of clear thinking and a unified path to godliness. As worship straightens us out as individuals, our marriages become less complicated and convoluted.

Worship also gives our marriages strength. Why does Paul say that God strengthens us according to the gospel and preaching (Rom. 16:25)? Because without it, we are unable to withstand temptation, unable to clearly see our way, unable to love as we should. Without it, we wither. Without it, a marriage cannot expect lasting happiness. With it, God has promised His blessing, and part of that is being able to, as a couple, run and not grow weary, walk and not grow faint.

And worship itself gives joy. There is great happiness in going together to a service: "I was glad when they said to me, 'Let us go to the house of the Lord!' Our feet have been standing within your gates, O Jerusalem!" (Ps. 122:1–2). If you are a Christian, you know that doing what you were created to do with the person closest to you is a happiness all its own—a foretaste of eternity and the worship that we will rejoice in without end or sin. The next time you are able to publicly pray, give, sing, and listen to the preached Word with a spouse, take it as a gift from the Lord, partly for the happiness of your marriage.

God created us for worship because, in it, we become increasingly reflective of His Son's image. Paul reminds us in 2 Corinthians, "We all, with unveiled face, beholding the glory of the Lord, are being transformed into the same image from one degree of glory to another" (3:18). Worship allows us to join in the praise of heaven while we are still on this earth. It changes our marriages in ways that nothing else can. "We receive the Spirit by the preaching of the gospel (Acts 2:33). . . . Where the Spirit of God is, there is liberty and purity and holiness."[11] To make the happiness in that clear, John Owen elaborates: "Holiness is nothing but the word changed into grace in our hearts. . . . All our thoughts, desires and actions are to be regulated by God's word."[12] Christian marriage begins with worship, and as a spouse passes into glory, it also ends in worship. Worship regulates our marriages. For God's children, the blessing that this brings to a marriage is, over time, inescapable.

Worship is also a reminder that our greatest happiness can never be in each other because we are limited and unable to meet each other's deepest needs. Worship reminds us not to seek ultimate satisfaction in each other. The joy of a happy marriage is a blessing flowing out of the greater blessing of knowing God, and worship reminds us of this above all else: our chief end is not to enjoy each other, but to enjoy God. Bernard of Clairvaux reminds us that Jesus is the source of joy for loving hearts: "From the best bliss that earth imparts we turn unfilled to thee again."[13] And worship allows us to be filled and then to overflow into our marriages and beyond.

Story (1977)

Bart and Nancie have lived in several cultures within the United States. Nancie took the time to answer these questions.

How did you meet?

We met on a blind date. It was love at first sight (for me, at least). He was a bit taken with me as well, I presume, since he invited me home to meet his parents the next day. It was a fairy-tale romance. We never saw each other upset until after our engagement. We talked on the phone every night for hours. On our wedding day, we had known each other for twenty weeks.

Do you have a happy marriage?

It depends on how you define *happy*. Webster's dictionary has some positive definitions, among them "enjoying or characterized by well-being or contentment." In today's world, the word *happy* is so poorly and inaccurately defined. Am *I* satisfied? Do *I* have what *I* want? Are things going *my* way?

If the approach to the question is, "Am I in the place/relationship/marriage where *God* has placed me and ordained for my life journey, good, sanctification, and ultimately His glory?" then *yes*, we have a "happy" marriage.

How do you know that your marriage is happy?

We have a happy marriage because we know that we are in the Lord's will in bringing us together the way He did and how we stand on the foundation and commitment of our marriage vows. I have never doubted Bart or whether our marriage was too hasty or a mistake. I have never questioned our trust in one another. And we have always known that our marriage is a lifelong journey of growing and serving together in the work the Lord has given us to do. When we fall off the rails, we get back on and continue the journey.

We have learned to recognize the strengths and weaknesses in each other's makeup and personalities. We respect one another. We recognize the integrity in one another. We have total trust in each other, even when we view things differently. We are resting in God's provision for each other as life partners.

One of the sweet things we have learned over the decades is recognizing that the characteristics or habits that were once annoyances to each other are now endearments and sweet affections as we have learned to recognize and live with each other's quirks.

What makes your marriage happy?

Our shared faith in Scripture. Our shared goals in raising our family, though coming from very different family backgrounds: Bart from a Christian family and raised in church, me from a secular family where I attended church periodically alone and came to faith at age twenty-one.

We realize that we are two sinners under one roof committed to working together to have a solid marriage. When Bart proposed, he told me that the word or thought of divorce was not an option. So from the beginning, our marriage was a lifelong commitment regardless of potholes that we might encounter along the way of our life journey together.

God and faith first, church (not to the exclusion of family needs and responsibilities), then marriage/spouse, then children, then extended family, and then work.

Has it always been happy?

From my perspective, no. But this thought is a reflection on my earlier immaturity as a believer and unrealistic expectations of what makes a marriage. We both needed to grow in our understanding of priorities now that we were no longer single and our schedules no longer affected not only ourselves, as well as priorities related to extended family. We both had to learn what it means for a man (or woman) to leave his (or her) father and mother and cleave to his wife (or husband).

How did that change?

Recognizing where we each fall short in our expectations and biblical responsibilities within a marriage.

Recognizing how differently we were viewing relationships with our different families of origin, our parents, and how we needed to recognize ourselves as a new family unit that needed to be prioritized, especially with Bart's traveling for work.

Recognizing how our differing views of the path we must take to arrive at common goals (children, work, service, social life, etc.)

were affecting our decisions. We worked on trying to get on the same page. I was determined to try to understand and live in the submissive, biblical role as a wife under the headship of my husband. Bart was learning to lead with gentleness and understanding.

What things have you found detract from happiness in your marriage?

Unrealized expectations when I dwell on them (don't make them idols) and unrealized life dreams (again, don't make them idols). Not being intentional in setting mutual goals and purpose, especially early on. Differing in the way that we organize our thoughts, desires, and expectations.

In raising children, balancing biblical guidance and discipline with the screams of worldly influence and distractions in the middle of current societal false gods.

Some things more pronounced in our later years. Indecision, mainly during our later years in a semiretirement status. Expectations of how to maintain a healthy lifestyle (eating, exercise, social interactions, use of our free time). Realizing that we have different interests or ways of relaxing.

How do you deal with remaining sin in yourselves in marriage?

Confession, prayer, calling on God's grace and work in sanctification in ourselves first and then our spouse. Remembering that we are not each other's holy spirit; let the true Holy Spirit do the work in each other that only He can do. Allowing God to reveal our heart's sinful ways and recognizing the log in our own eye first. Refusing to accuse each other: trying to raise issues of concern at the proper time and in a proper manner with respect for the other.

Knowing that there will always be remaining sin in each of our lives as long as we are here on earth. This will always be a work in progress as the Lord uses each of us in His work of sanctifying the other.

What things have you noticed that drain happiness?

Different lacks. A lack of communication, which can keep us guessing what the other is thinking. Lack of oneness or unity on an issue. Lack of intentionality in marriage and family direction and how to reach mutual goals. A lack of intimacy in various ways—not just in the physical relationship but in time together while focusing on one another as husband and wife without distractions from the day's issues (work, children, cultural concerns, extended-family issues, etc.).

In ministry, the 24/7 demands on a husband are hard. There is a need to understand the sacrificial level of service in preparation and work that gospel ministry requires of both spouses.

Self-centeredness, self-pity, clinging to lost dreams, regret, desiring control.

Are there habits or patterns that help establish happiness?

We are still working on them. Unfortunately, we got off to a weak beginning because of Bart's extensive weekly travel schedule. We never had that early time of setting patterns for daily living together and so had inconsistent patterns that did not work for both of us together as a unit. This caused conflict because we were not communicating our concerns but still living and thinking independently.

There are some things that can be done to set a positive tone in a marriage before poor habits set in. Early on, establishing the primary roles of husband and wife and making sure that this relationship takes precedence over others (vs. child, sibling, parent, etc.). The husband needs to work with his wife to establish what he is delegating to her (keeping track of money, child-rearing/discipline, etc.).

If there are children, both parents need to stand united in front of them. They need to back each other up in decisions concerning the children. Discuss differences of opinion privately.

Intentionally set aside time to set goals for the marriage and the children, and determine how you desire to meet those goals. Periodically review and adjust as needed.

Set boundaries around the marriage, to not allow overindulgent or intrusive or critical parents to create wedges between husband and wife. This does not mean excluding them from your lives, but protect the covenantal status of your own God-created and God-ordained family unit.

Because of the nature of schedules that rarely follow a set routine in ministry, we have adjusted to this pattern in our marriage. I guess the answer is flexibility.

Continue to pursue each other as you did before marriage.

Who are your marriage role models?

To some degree, my unbelieving parents. Their appropriate outward affection toward one another and their lack of disagreement in front of the children made me feel secure in knowing/believing that my parents' marriage was solid when I saw my friends' parents' marriages in disarray and often breaking up. I also saw how they valued the family as a whole by not letting one member get so involved in a personal activity that kept the family from enjoying life together (such as ballet, Little League, horses, soccer, travel teams, etc.): things that took over the family schedule and dictated family time, especially on weekends. Looking back and comparing this attitude to today's overscheduled children's activities that may rob families of regular family time, regular dinner together, shared family interests, etc., I am grateful. Our shared family interest growing up was sailing: all four children could participate in various ways. These things are the positives.

To some degree, my husband's parents, in the way that they were united even in their quirkiness. They enjoyed common activities and social interactions together while comfortably having their own personal activities. Their ties to a local church provided relationship opportunities of leadership and fellowship in church and community. I saw their love for their two sons and how they continued to show genuine interest in their welfare as they became grown men with their own families. A very important thing I saw regularly was their sense of humor and ability to laugh. But the thing that stands out most to me is Bart's father's integrity. I see where my husband gets his immense quality of integrity. He was raised by a father who demonstrated integrity to the utmost degree in all he did.

A couple with whom we worked when we were younger were also models. Jane was a godly woman, very mature in her faith. She modeled a submissive spirit under the headship of her godly husband, Tom, in a cheerful, joyful manner. She relinquished a career for a move that benefited her husband and family, relocating away from her family and friends. Because she walked with the Lord from a very early age, she began her marriage on a strong foundation with a good understanding of it.

We all need to think generationally about how we are passing on the truth of God's Word in how to live faithfully in the covenantal relationships that the Lord has ordained for our sanctification and joy. Unfortunately, we don't always recognize these qualities in those who go before us when we are young and idealistic, yearning to be independent. Gray-haired wisdom is acquired through years of trial and suffering, growing in knowledge, understanding, and a deeper walk of faith to help us see what this life is about—glorifying God and enjoying Him forever. Being vulnerable and willing to seek the counsel and wisdom of godly couples who have moved beyond the idealistic stage of early marriage is so important.

Can you share one story that shaped your relationship or made you think differently about your spouse?

As I mentioned, early in our marriage Bart traveled Monday through Friday for work. I taught during the day and went to school at night to get my master's. At the end of a week shortly after Bart returned, we were both tired and a bit short-tempered. We were impatient with each other, not listening or understanding the exhausting week that the other had come through. I was heating up a can of peas for dinner, and there was disagreement over how I was doing it. "How can you mess up a can of peas?" I thought. I exploded, out of proportion to the issue at hand. Bart brought me back to reality, saying, "We went through your cancer holding each other together by our faith, so why are we falling apart over a can of peas?" The absurdity of the disagreement brought us back in focus.

That episode comes to mind frequently when I find myself overreacting to nonsense issues that Satan loves to exaggerate to the extreme, trying to cause division in our marriage by tempting me/us to selfish, sinful desires, reactions, pity parties. It made me realize that although we often come at things differently, I respect my husband's authority and wisdom, knowing that he is trying to faithfully fulfill his role as my head with great responsibility before the Lord to do so. We will both stand before the Lord to give an account, he as to how he fulfilled his calling as husband, me for how I obeyed and fulfilled my role as helpmeet to the man given to me by God Himself.

How do you live with sadness in a good marriage?

We have both had critical brushes with cancer. Both of our experiences strengthened our faith and dependence on a holy and sovereign heavenly Father. We grew in our understanding of God's providences in our lives: how He has a purpose in them to bring us closer to Him by faith and trust, accepting whatever He chooses to use in our lives for our growth and sanctification. Even now, the Lord uses these experiences to grow our marriage in trust, obedience, compassion, understanding, and patience with each other. The residual physical and emotional effects of cancer can alter a number of things in the life of a cancer survivor and their spouse. This is true of many health issues.

Other sadnesses have been two early miscarriages, the loss of all four parents, my brother's sudden death at age sixty-six, job issues, disappointments in work relationships.

We live with them through acceptance, knowing that God is sovereign and has purposefully placed these issues in our lives for our good and His glory. He is working in the lives of everyone involved, even when it hurts. Our response of faith is a testimony to others of a trustworthy heavenly Father.

We realize that as a couple, we may be at different places in processing disappointments, giving each other space, time, and support as we process these events in our own way. Prayer is essential:

knowing that God hears us and is attentive to His sheep. We can pour out our hearts to Him in our weakness and sorrow. He knows our hearts and our pain.

By faithfully putting one foot in front of the other and continuing to live in the light of God's providences, knowing that He is in control and provides strength to persevere in what He calls us to do. Even when we don't feel His presence, we know that He is with us by faith.

By believing God's Word. He will do and is doing what He says He will do in the lives of His people.

By looking forward to God's promises to be fulfilled in eternity and knowing that the struggle of life's journey here on earth is only a blip on the radar with God's purpose of glorifying Himself as He sanctifies His people through our joys, disappointments, and sufferings to bring us—His chosen people—to Himself in heaven.

How have complicating factors shaped your marriage?

Difficult relationships made us realize more and more the sinfulness of man and the self-serving nature of some. We try not to sink into sinful thought and response patterns and reactions, but seek the Lord's counsel through prayer, and also search our hearts for the logs in our own eyes first.

With challenging physical changes and illness, we have had to let dreams and earthly desires go. But in this we have gained understanding of our future hope with Christ in eternity, where all will be made new. We have gained an understanding of the strength of our marriage vows to love each other in sickness and health, for richer, for poorer, and in all challenges through life we are one together in the Lord.

Challenging issues in adult children's lives/families can be a difficult struggle. They are no longer under our authority, and we take care not to intrude but instead offer lots of encouragement and lots and lots of prayer together for their welfare and God's provision. We have been empty-nesters for more than twenty years, no longer working for income, and the weight of family issues seems to be more prominent. Now that we are not juggling work schedules and so many daily needs that come with raising children, there is more thought to our children's family issues now and their futures in a dramatically changing world. Prayer is a priority, letting them know of our support and availability to help if needed. We trust that they are in the Lord's hands.

We are also at the stage of anticipating our possible need for assistance from children as we get older. Trying to determine what is best to enable our children to be of assistance without burdening them more than necessary, seeing different outlooks on things because of their different spiritual conditions and locations—again, with much prayer and gentle probing of our children's thinking on these issues.

All this to say, we lean on each other more with deeper understanding. We are more aware that the other processes things differently but always know that we are standing on the same foundation: Jesus Christ. We encourage each other more and more as we understand each other's way of thinking and needs. We realize more and more where our strength comes from—the Lord.

What advantages has age given your marriage?

Patience with each other. There is more selflessness and less selfishness. Loving each other in a much deeper, less superficial way. We are more caring and compassionate toward each other. We are able to accept what is, not what we want, dreamed of, or desired.

We have been able to see God work faithfully in the life circumstances that He placed on our path in the midst of marriage and family. He is faithful to do what He says He will do, in His way and timing. We begin to see and understand more of His purpose in the midst of His providences, rather than after the fact, both positive and challenging. Even when we don't understand, we know that He is working for our benefit.

We have a greater and deeper biblical understanding of God's divine plan in all of life and His creation ordinance of marriage. Before, we may have had the knowledge of God's design, but now we have experienced that design through our shared life experience and struggles. We see and take our wedding vows more seriously and with greater understanding of the power of those vows made before the Lord—and His continuing help with keeping and honoring those vows made to each other.

We have seen God's faithfulness in answered prayer. We can look back and see His perfect plan in how He brought us together. We had prayed fervently that He would prevent our marriage if we were not pursuing it under His divine will. God kept us on the right path as we navigated the bumps and potholes along the road.

We know that God's hand is in everything in our lives together, and He will never let us go. He will finish what He has begun in each of our lives and as a covenantal unit.

What challenges did you not expect, and how did you navigate them?

Unexpected corners of each other's personalities—possibly a result of such a brief time between our meeting and our marriage. At the same time, though, most young couples don't know the questions to ask before marriage.

My greatest unexpected challenge was understanding my in-laws and their over-involvement and interest in our marriage and decisions. In retrospect, I now understand that it was their way of showing love and concern. But they did not understand our need to be a separate unit and to set our own way of maintaining our marriage.

It was difficult to consistently work on issues with Bart's travel, and he was not there to shelter me from the over-concerns of his mother, which at the time he did not recognize. With Bart's approval, I sought out counseling, which created great concern when his parents found out. In retrospect, it was God's providence, because it created an opportunity for Bart to set some specific boundaries around our brief times together on weekends.

Over time, we worked on changing our expectations as our life trajectory changed dramatically when the decision was made to go to seminary, go into ministry, and move away from family. This distance meant that we were each other's primary confidants, and were away from intrusive, unsolicited advice, however well intentioned. We finally began to engage as a separate family unit. We did not sever relationships with our parents. The change just reflected new biblical priorities in our marriage. Our parents needed to learn this as well.

After three years of marriage and moving nine hundred miles away for more than twenty years, I was able to really be a wife and not compete with my mother-in-law. I began to grow in my own confidence to be a loving wife and mother in my own way, using the gifts that God had given me, which were somewhat different from my mother-in-law's. The move gave me time to grow up, and once I became a mother, I began to grasp some understanding of her devotion and opinions. I slowly began to learn to let it all go and leave our differences in the Lord's hands, learning to appreciate the strengths and wisdom that she had to offer, which were significant.

In the end, Bart's mother and I grew to love and honor one another and serve one another in a more accepting and respectful manner. I physically cared for her during illnesses and spent her final weeks and days with her before her death. Those were sweet times of healing and forgiving for both of us. Today I honor her for her role in raising up such a wonderful, godly man to be my husband.

Trying to understand the purpose that God has in putting these unexpected challenges into our marriage made us grow and changed us to enable us to trust Him by faith and change us into His likeness.

What blessing did you not expect that God has given your marriage?

The integrity found in a good marriage, not just the joy of a lifelong companion. Having a partner in the journey of growing consistency in persevering to the end goal of glorifying God. Also our efforts in obeying His Word about faithfulness in a biblical marriage.

God uses marriage as a primary means to work in us our sanctification. Iron sharpens iron. Even when rough edges clash, He is perfecting us and making us holy through marriage.

Growth in understanding how hard life's brief journey on this sin-filled earth is. And growth in our understanding of who God is and what His purpose is and how He works out His plan in our lives. It is not about me, my spouse, our family. It is all about God and His glorious purpose to create and redeem a people of His choosing for

His purpose and glory alone, through the finished work of His Son, Jesus Christ, on the cross.

What has your marriage been able to do because it is happy?

We have been able to minister together in seminary and church employment, which has given us the opportunity to counsel others together through various life struggles, marriages, family, illness, death, discouragement, new babies, etc., from our own life experiences, relying on the power of God's Word and His faithfulness to us.

Hopefully, our imperfect marriage is a visual example to others of a faithful and loving marriage carried out according to the creation mandate: one man, one woman until death do us part. I especially want my unbelieving family and friends to see us carry out God's design of marriage as a covenant before God, never to be broken.

What encouragement would you give to someone in an unhappy marriage?

God placed you in this marriage by design. Be patient and watch expectantly to see God's work for your spouse's and your sanctification.

Search your heart to ask why you are unhappy. Is it because you do not have what you want? Is your spouse not doing what you want, or doing what you don't want them to do? Are things not going the way that you want? Is your unhappiness all about you? What attitudes can you change to improve the level of happiness or contentment with the marriage? Have you considered what your spouse might be struggling with? How can you reach out and begin to communicate and address each other's desire for a better and happier marriage? Do you have appropriate expectations of your marriage, spouse, and self?

Be a testimony to others by how you live and respond in your difficult and lonely situation. React to your unhappiness by your faith in the Lord's goodness and presence with you as you are faithful to your vows in spite of unhappiness.

God sees and knows your need. He is faithful and is working in you and through you to make you holy and is enabling you to do the work—the marriage—that He has given you until He brings you to your Bridegroom in heaven.

What is your favorite thing about being married?

I know that my husband is always there and is not going anywhere. We have a wonderful level of trust between us. Trust in the big and little things, the important things that matter to us in our bond of marriage.

I love the intimate and personal understanding known only to us (except God) and between us. And the secret signals of our affection, love, and support for each other.

I frequently reflect on my initial response that brought my heart to know that Bart was a blessing from God dropped into my lap unexpectedly to be my life partner. It was so clear and unquestioned. Those same qualities and more are still very much present in his character and in our marriage. I have never doubted Bart's faithfulness to and love for me, or the Lord's bringing us together. Psalm 121: Hallelujah!

10

Time

Sarah lived 127 years;
these were the years of the life of Sarah.
And Sarah died at Kiriath-arba (that is, Hebron)
in the land of Canaan, and Abraham went in to mourn
for Sarah and to weep for her.
—Genesis 23:1–2

For something that is so familiar, time is something that we do not really understand. Perhaps its very familiarity leads us to underestimate and underappreciate what it is and thus what it does. Time can be an ally or an enemy. Occasionally, it is both. So often, we feel it working against us: we try to save time, lose track of time, waste time, and even kill time. We feel its effect on our bodies and minds as we age. Too often, we feel most keenly what time takes: opportunities, abilities, chances, health, loved ones. Every marriage is shadowed by the reality of the relationship's eventual end. The happier the marriage, the darker that cloud can look. The joy of a marriage is limited, bound by time.

But God has placed our marriages within time—and He did so before the fall, so this is not a result of the curse, although it is affected by it. Souls are not limited to the dimensions of this world, but particular human relationships are, including the closest ones. That is not accidental. Because time is part of God's good creation, we can experience the happiness that God gives through time in our marriages. In a Christian marriage, time is on our side.

John Archibald Wheeler, one of America's most influential physicists, wrote, "Space-time tells matter how to move; matter tells space-time how to curve."[1] It's a mind-bending idea, that time and space are interconnected and can be shaped by sheer mass. Equally profound is the concept that God uses time and space to control the movement of planets and massive stars. As an idea, time is beyond us. Scripture tells us that time is itself a created thing, and that there will be a day when time itself will cease.[2] While we live with it in this world, time bends and shapes our relationships, just as it does the universe. Wheeler would know: he and his wife were married for seventy-two years before her death.

Because time permeates our current existence, we often fail to see the effects that it has on our relationships. When a couple get married, they promise to be faithful "till death do us part." This is love for the long haul. For marriage—especially a Christian marriage—time is a gift. Though it does eventually remove strength, energy, health, and other abilities, God uses time to give even more than it takes. And just as it helps shape the universe, time certainly shapes our marriages and brings happiness to them.

Perhaps the most basic happiness that time gives a marriage is the open opportunity to show someone how much you love him or her. Day after day, you can express to a spouse how dear he or she is to you, in word, action, and attitude. Time and affection go together.

Simply being together, doing life at the same time in shared spaces, creates a unity. Our lives become intertwined, tangled together in a way that binds—one reason that divorce is so painful. If you are married to another Christian, this synchronization is a good thing. And its effects are measurable. Social psychologist James Pennebaker points out, "The more we spend time with other people, the more our identity becomes fused with them." This even changes our vocabulary: seniors statistically use the word *we* far more and the word *I* far less than teens, showing that, for better or worse, we do adopt a group identity as we age.[3] The closer and longer the relationship, the greater the effect.

But this is not simply inevitable statistics. It is a measurement that reflects marriage's design. We are supposed to grow closer over time, to think more as one than as two. Because we are naturally self-focused and self-directed, this is not a natural process. God gives us the gift of time as a significant part of what enables us to learn thinking, speaking, and living in a way that is other-focused. Time fosters harmonization. People do not usually find soulmates: instead, we become them.

There is a deeply personal aspect to time. Time allows us to know each other—to amass a body of knowledge about another person. The ability to know how someone thinks and feels enables us to better care for that person, but especially to enjoy what we are learning and understanding. Robert Browning looked back at his early marriage and said, "Why, time was what I wanted, to turn o'er / Within my mind each look, get more and more / By heart each word, too much to learn at first."[4] Time gives us space to savor each other.

But time also teaches us new things about our spouses. Time gives us room to truly understand each other by observation and meditation. It allows us to predict—at least much of the time!—responses to situations and stresses. Watching our husbands and wives go through different life stages allows us to learn more about them as people, as they deal with different situations and phases, from night feedings to financial stresses to wedding planning to caring for dying parents to walking through terminal illness: personality can unfold more fully. Time allows us to watch how the Lord brings them through sad or difficult things and to see how His faithfulness has shaped them for His glory. Time gives us the blessing of seeing our spouses grow in grace, seeing them increasingly become the people that God made them to be. What a joy that is, to look back together on life and remember how immature and unwise we were at the beginning, and to thank the Lord for where He has brought us.

Because time gives the opportunity to know our spouses better, we are able to love them more. The longer we look at other Christians, and the more they progress in sanctification, the more there is in them to love. One older man I knew described this as a binder he kept in his mind, his wife's name on the cover, full of pages and files about her likes and preferences and abilities so that he could better love her and work with her. The selflessness that Christian marriage fosters overflows to other relationships as we learn to consider others first and to outdo one another in showing honor. This inevitably brings relational blessing.

Stretches of married time also give us a bank of blessings to enjoy, a list of the Lord's goodnesses experienced jointly. One of the fun things about marriage is the vast history of shared adventures to enjoy in the moment and also to look back on. The ability to say,

"Remember when . . ." and bring a smile to a spouse's face is one of the joys that God designed time to give us. The longer the marriage, the bigger this happiness becomes.

By giving us shared experiences, time also gives a sort of similarity. This is different from harmony and sameness, and does not mean simply that we can reminisce about the same things: it means that the same things have shaped us. There is something profound about this design element. The Armenian Genocide of 1915 forced David Kheridan's mother out of her country, away from her family, and into a new world and life. In his memoir of her experience, Kheridan writes of the internal divisions that the external pressures created in the family: "I didn't understand at first why we were so changed, because I had always thought that blood was such a strong tie, but as time went on, it became clearer to me that what separated people—or brought them together—was the way they responded to their experiences."[5] If two people are being shaped by the same Word and worship in the same direction through a shared life, then time will allow them to respond in similar ways to their shared experiences, further facilitating oneness. "Emotions," writes social psychologist Pennebaker, "are not just reactions to events. . . . Emotions are intensely social in that they can draw us closer together or push us farther apart."[6] The accumulated time of shared life really can bind a couple together as they look at life the same way partly because of the trials that they have come through together. Even as distinct individuals, a husband and wife will take on similar attitudes toward life, what it brings to them, and what it brings them through.

Time also allows us to solve problems that we face, not only in marriage but in life together in this world. Albert Einstein said that the ability to solve a problem is not primarily intellectual prowess but mostly the ability to keep thinking about it long enough for a solution to open up. If relativity can be cracked by time to think, so can the issues facing a marriage. Time spent patiently talking, being in the Word, and thinking through different angles can solve a myriad of problems that cannot be fixed in the moment.

Sometimes we do not even see that a problem is there—an irritant or issue creates friction that we do not initially feel simply because it has always been there and we have not had the time to recognize it and realize the need for the right change. It takes time to find and work out the bugs in a marriage, and just for this reason, time can bring great blessing.

Connected to this is the development of trust. A missionary told my husband that his mantra on the field was this: "Love is freely given; trust is earned." While this is a useful thought for gospel ministry, it is also true in a marriage. Falling in love can be effortless and instant; gaining trust is not. Trust needs time to build. Time gives us space to earn it—increasingly with greater responsibilities and greater risks. Budgeting to pay off student debt is a step toward earning trust with mortgages and credit cards. Having filtering software on phones and computers is a step toward building trust in fidelity. Maintaining healthy routines such as Bible reading through sickness or other disruptions creates trust in character and priorities. Long patterns of faithfulness in the little things spawn trust for the big things when they come. While no spouse is infallible, we can show ourselves to be worthy of trust in different aspects of life as we accumulate a history of faithfulness over time.

Because it allows trust, knowledge, and other aspects to develop, time necessarily grows the strength of a Christian marriage. A mature marriage can bear things that an immature one could not. Maybe it is the death of someone who was close to you both; perhaps the apostasy of a child; a diagnosis; loss of a job; a church split—many situations and experiences can be a body blow to a relationship. A marriage that has had time to be grounded in the Word, to put down relational roots, to be synchronized, will not be toppled by these things. Pain may come, but it will not take away stability and peace with each other.

Perhaps the greatest happiness that time gives a marriage, though, is maturity. The maturity "of a fully-developed Christian character, expressing itself in consistent Christian living, . . . requires time and patient progress."[7] God uses time, often paired with suffering, to bring us the happiness of a mature relationship. Time grows a couple out of what Anthony Trollope called "hobbledehoyhood": "they are not as yet men, whatever the number may be of their years; . . . [they are] unripe fruit."[8] Time ripens our marriages. Time allows our marriages to be fruit that is ready to feed others through the stability and wisdom that maturity gives.

There are different aspects to maturity. Time is a great giver of emotional maturity. Perhaps you have seen a young couple at the front of a church, expressing their love to one another in a wedding ceremony. Of course they love each other, but it is a love that is often shallow, untested, unknowing—inexperienced compared with what it will be in a few decades. Time allows that love to become deepened by responsibility, as it learns to bear weight. Love is balanced by experience, as we know each other better and learn to love better. And love is matured by trials that not only test love but so often require costly expressions of that love. This sort of love is steady and deep, enabling a couple to bear much together as they are buoyed by each other's support and affection.

There is also relational maturity. Children are born thinking that the world revolves around them, and part of growing up is realizing that it does not and being content with that reality. So often, marriage takes this realization to another level, as our own selfishness and relational immaturity are exposed by intimacy. Living with someone who is not a parent or child, and who shares everything down to the bed, forces a spouse to consider the other person's needs, likes, and opinions on a new level. In happy marriages, we learn to do this so that we think of our spouses' preferences and needs as often as our own—instinctively. This is also a gift that God gives over time, often through pain, from the small pain of not getting our own way, to the deep pain of significant suffering. Jane Austen describes the immaturity of a character at the beginning of *Mansfield Park* and contrasts this self-centeredness with his change at the novel's end: "He had suffered, and he had learned to think, two advantages that he had never known before. . . . He became what he ought to be: . . . not merely living for himself."[9] Painful though it may be, this kind of maturation does bring happiness to a marriage.

Relational maturity extends to the happiness of children and grandchildren: the maturity of simply being the older people in the family. In his *Sketches*, Charles Dickens describes the joy that an old couple receive from having children and grandchildren around them: "The old couple sit side by side, and the old time seems like yesterday indeed. Looking back upon the path they have travelled, its dust and ashes disappear; the flowers that withered long ago, show brightly again upon its borders, and they grow young once more in the youth of those about them."[10] This happiness is actually something that Scripture notes, too, as it repeatedly connects seeing grandchildren with covenantal blessing and joy. A mature older couple are a source of wisdom and stability to the family and community around them, providing wisdom and example, yes, but an overflow of love that brings encouragement and support to those fortunate enough to experience it.

Of all the aspects of maturity that time brings to a Christian marriage, spiritual maturity must bring the most joy. The worship, Scripture reading, prayer—the fellowship with God—create in believers a Christlikeness so that even as time brings them closer together, they are increasingly remade in the image of the Lord Jesus. Even as believing spouses learn to fit together better, care for each other, and give the help and companionship that we need in this life, their dependence is increasingly on the Lord. In a happy marriage, spouses become very close, but in a happy Christian marriage, this closeness is outstripped by a love for the Lord as time makes each spouse more like Christ than like the other. This aspect of happiness is ironic: maturity does not bring independence but brings an increasing dependence on the right Source. The closeness to Christ that a Christian marriage fosters is a joy that continues beyond the relationship.

This is part of the sadness of a short marriage—it is robbed of the happiness that time can give, the happiness of being "more tender, more tried, more fixed in a knowledge of each other's character, truth and attachment; more equal to act, more justified in acting."[11] Lengthened years, as Hannah Gould writes, really are a gift.[12]

But then, a long marriage brings its own pain: that very closeness that a marriage gains over time is what makes the death of a spouse difficult, isn't it? Decades of growing together make the tearing apart more painful. But they also make it beautiful.

Have you witnessed the ending of a happy marriage? Have you seen the increasing tenderness in the face of illness, the gentle care responding to disability and pain, the intensifying love that seems defiant in the face of the last, inevitable enemy—death? It is a difficult thing to watch, partly because it is so beautiful. There are few things like death to show something for what it is, and a happy marriage facing this curse brings a glory into the horror because it is borrowing from the glory of eternity. As a picture of Christ and His church, a marriage that is in Christ can actually say: "O death, where is your victory? O death, where is your sting?" (1 Cor. 15:55). When death ends a marriage, the happiness is not in the marriage, but in Christ: "'Death is swallowed up in victory.' . . . Thanks be to God, who gives us the victory through our Lord Jesus Christ" (vv. 54, 57).

And Scripture seems to indicate that part of the blessing of a Christian marriage is preparation for dying. In explaining the reality of marriage to the Sadducees, Jesus points out that there is no marrying or being given in marriage in heaven because "they cannot die anymore . . . , being sons of the resurrection" (Luke 20:35–36). In a world where everyone dies, Christian marriage gives the great happiness not only of help in sanctification over a lifetime but also help and encouragement for a spouse who is dying. Because we will not need those helps in eternity, marriage becomes superfluous—redundant as college studies or a good doctor would be in glory.

The end of a happy marriage brings an entirely new phase of life for the surviving spouse. It does not leave a bachelor, but a widower; not a single woman, but a widow. Our very vocabulary notes the mark that marriage leaves on a person. In her novel *Wives and Daughters*, Elizabeth Gaskell shows an old man adjusting to his new identity of widower: "'We've been so much taken up thinking about you. I don't know what's come over me to speak of "we"—"we" in this way,' said he, suddenly dropping his voice,—a change of tone as sad as sad could be. 'I ought to say "I;" it will be "I" for evermore in this world.'"[13] The end of a happy marriage brings real and deep suffering. Augustine wrote that his partner of many years "was torn from my side. . . . My heart, which had fused with hers, was mutilated by the wound, and I limped along trailing blood."[14] Oneness has its cost.

Though there will be gratitude for the marriage, happiness in good memories and joy in the fruit that it brought, death places bounds on that earthly happiness. That marriage cannot create new happiness, but the joy and blessing of the glorified spouse is full. In Christ, even in the darkest time of a happy marriage, there is resurrection hope and the promise of future communion, as well as thanks for what the Lord did through marriage in this life. And for the Christian, the cost of love and grief is not the end. A new oneness waits for the end of our time in this world. The best really is yet to be.

Writing to her husband, Caroline Noel models biblical thinking about both the joy of a marriage and its end:

> One on Christ's bosom gently laid,
> The other safely led
> A longer road, unto the land
> Where live the blessed dead. . . .
> O deep unspeakable repose
> Of knowing, that for aye
> All that disturbed and hindered love
> Has wholly passed away! . . .
> Sin, sickness, sorrow, chills of age,
> And pangs of mortal fear,
> Can never reach the land where Christ
> Has wiped away each tear.

For Death has no dominion there,
Where Sin has never trod,
But souls transfigured, live and love,
Within the life of God.
Then fear we not to trust His Word,
And cherish love's increase;
Since e'en its sharpest throes
Must pass into eternal peace.[15]

The fact that death will bring grief should never allow us to hold back emotionally in a marriage. Fuller, freer love does bring deeper, sharper loss, but this is also something under the Lord's control and stewardship, and in His economy it is always a valuable investment.

Perhaps death gives us the greatest perspective on a happy marriage, as we see it in its completion and feel its full effect. To paraphrase James Stalker, marriage is measured by results. Was it good for my spouse that I was his or her spouse? "In the maturity of his fully-formed judgement will he look back on the connection with approval? At the judgement seat and eternity will he prize it?"[16] When God gives His blessing to a marriage, the happiness will extend beyond this time in which we live now. We will fully see how God used it when we see each other in glory at the final reunion.

Story (1983)

Four continents and multiple languages, moves, and ministry positions have shaped Henry and Eleanor's marriage. They currently serve in an Eastern European country through pastoral ministry, evangelism, hospitality, mentoring younger missionaries, and more. These thoughts come through Eleanor's voice.

Do you have a happy marriage?

Maybe "joy" would be a better description of our marriage. Joy is steadfast. It persists as a tenuous thread throughout difficult times because of the unfailing grace of our Savior. It is truthfully a struggle to write about marriage—it is not clean and tidy. What comes to mind are so many times of personal failure, doubt, and sinfulness messily mixed in with decades of a loving marriage and fruitful ministry. Certainly, there have been periods of wonderful happiness, but honestly, there have also been times of weary struggle.

What makes your marriage happy?

Do you remember the narrative of the birth of Jesus: an unplanned pregnancy, disgrace, a long journey, pain, displacement, and homelessness? Throughout it all, joy persisted. Mary exclaimed, "My spirit rejoices in God my Savior" (Luke 1:47). The angels shouted news of great joy to startled shepherds despite the impending cruelty of Herod. Joy had little relation to circumstances, places, people, or personal emotions. It had to do with a Savior. That is true for us.

Has it always been happy?

The context of our marriage has been ministry from first to last. We met at seminary, and our relationship grew out of an initial compatibility, friendship, and shared interests. For Henry, it was love at first sight, an instant connection or recognition of a kindred spirit.

But I had many insecurities and a lack of maturity that required more time and reassurance. For me, deep friendship and goodness of character were my first attraction to Henry. Once we began a relationship, our interactions were perhaps a little scandalous on a very conservative seminary campus. It was springtime, and I remember a lot of laughter, affection, sweetness, and joy. In some ways, I think it was a refreshing offset to a very circumspect and reserved community. It still makes me smile to think of it.

That initial joy has overall persisted over these years in a shared sense of purpose, camaraderie, humor, affection, and partnership in family and ministry. There is a sense of humble wonder and deep fulfillment in seeing how the Lord has allowed us to participate in what He is doing wherever we have served. He has taken us on a life adventure side by side with the person we love. Sometimes we have looked at each other in amazement and exclaimed, "Who gets to have a life like we have?"

But there have also been times of real struggle along the way. Often, we have experienced God's training in righteousness that tested the limits of our faith. Often, I responded with immaturity and frustration. Yet God was willing to persist. What amazing grace and kindness.

What things have you found that detract from happiness in your marriage?

The obvious response to this is also the true response: sin. Self-centeredness is the most damaging and persistent sin for our marriage. Sometimes this sin starts to take shape in a person's early childhood if there is neglect or trauma. A deep belief forms that no one (including God) will really take care of me; I have to take care of myself. In adulthood, it becomes uglier. Despite experiencing the goodness of God, the loving people He has placed in my life, and the provision of every need, I still sometimes revert back to the belief that I have to take care of myself first.

How do you deal with remaining sin in yourselves in marriage?

One day at a time, one hour at a time. I have heard many senior believers say that the older they get, the more sinful they feel. When you reach age sixty or seventy, there is a huge accumulation of sins, large and small, in your past. Each day you have to believe the gospel again. Christ died for my sins. My life depends on that. An utter reliance on grace fosters humility, trust, and deep gratitude.

What things have you noticed that drain happiness?

So many things can drain our happiness: a critical spirit, begrudging service to each other, shut-down communication, disagreement on priorities and goals, rivalry, etc. Early on in our marriage, I struggled with a loss of a sense of identity. I had trained for ministry and had a master's degree. Suddenly I was no longer a single person with my own qualifications, desires, and goals. When we met people for the first time, they would turn to my husband and say, "And what work do you do?" I felt erased. It took time for "I" to become "we." A couple of verses that made an impact on me during this season were from 2 Corinthians 5:14–15: "For the love of Christ controls us, because we have concluded this: that one has died for all, therefore all have died; and he died for all, that those who live might no longer live for themselves but for him who for their sake died and was raised." My primary goal had to be knowing and living the love of Christ, which, by its very nature, was self-sacrificial.

Are there any habits or patterns that establish/perpetuate happiness?

At one point, we realized more deeply that there are certain aspects of God's character that human beings are not supposed to share. I am not sovereign. When I try to be in control, I will become stressed and anxious. I am not all-knowing. I need a humble and teachable heart. I am not able to be present everywhere at the same time. I have to let God take care of those who are far away. I am not all-powerful. There are things that are beyond my strength, but I can trust in God's strength. I am not infinite. I have limits. I am a created being, created with limitations that are designed to remind me that I am absolutely dependent on my Creator.

Understanding that we are human has been a huge help to our marriage. It reminds us to be patient, compassionate, and a suitable help to each other. It teaches us to laugh at mistakes and to get up when we fall down. It helps us give ownership of all things to God and rest in His work, purposes, and provision. We don't need to be strong and in control.

Who are your marriage role models?

Both of us grew up in the context of Christian community. There were many role models, none perfect, but all who loved and served Jesus. We learned that marriage isn't perfect. Each relationship has strengths and weaknesses, but in the fellowship of believers can be found all that is needed for wisdom, support, and encouragement.

Can you share one story or event that shaped or shifted your relationship, or made you think differently about it or your spouse?

One morning Henry took our four-year-old son outside to "help" him change the tire on the car. Together they jacked up the car. Henry held the lug wrench and let Max put his little hands in between. It was hot, exhausting work, and after it was over, Max dusted off his little hands and exclaimed proudly: "Look! I changed the tire on the car!" In that moment, we realized together that everything in ministry is the Lord's doing: the "car" belongs to Him, He fixes it according to His plan, and it is His strength and wisdom at work. And He is kind enough to include us as a couple in the joy and purposefulness of His work and mission.

How do you live with sadness in a good marriage?

On the mission field we came face-to-face with much injustice, trauma, sickness, poverty, and death. It could feel overwhelming and exhausting. A breakthrough in understanding and coping came as we began to understand better the nature of suffering and of "training in righteousness" (2 Tim. 3:16). Hebrews 2:10 talks about how, "in bringing many sons to glory," Jesus was made mature or complete through suffering.

He was prepared for ministry as a trusted High Priest by going through the same difficulties as His followers. They could draw close to Him and feel safe in His presence. It slowly became worth it to have gone through struggles. And we were able to have hope and give encouragement to those around us who were struggling.

How have "complicating factors" shaped your marriage?

After our two years of marriage as students at seminary and in a church internship, we spent the next twelve years as missionaries in an underdeveloped, unsafe area of the Middle East. Our three beautiful children were born there, and in many ways the ministry bore much fruit. But it was also exhausting. There was always more that could be done. There were obstacles, dangers, sickness, stress, and innumerable opportunities. We had to learn to balance family life and ministry life.

Another complicating factor in our marriage was that it was crosscultural. We were from very different cultures and backgrounds. We entered marriage with many diverse expectations. It took time and patience to listen to a different perspective and different values.

What challenges did you not expect, and how do you navigate them?

If we had understood our limitations as humans more deeply, earlier on in ministry, I believe that we would have been spared the experience of burnout. In those early years, we lived and ministered as though so much of it depended on us. We had a hard time setting limits and saying no; we pridefully overcommitted ourselves as though nothing would happen without us. We had to learn that there really is only one Savior of the world.

As the stress and exhaustion increased, unresolved struggles from the past snowballed into a profound depression for me. At the same time, Henry's father passed away from cancer. There were struggles in the local church, political upheaval, and terrorist threats. We made the decision that we would have to leave the Middle East. But even at this low point, God provided a powerful display of His love and sovereignty. Henry and the leaders on our team had been dealing with an unjust court case for several years. On the final day before the decision was to be handed down, several pastors came to Henry almost in despair. There was seemingly nothing left that could be done. They decided to spend that final night in prayer together, realizing that this was not ultimately a political battle but a spiritual one. The next day the judge who had been bribed was sick, and a replacement judge recognized the spuriousness of the case and threw it out of court. In God's mercy, He affirmed to our coworkers that even as we were leaving, it was God's church, and His power and plan would take it forward. God gave us the reassurance we needed at a difficult time of transition.

But my struggle with paralyzing depression was to continue for another three or four years, and it ultimately required that I start from the very beginning in understanding who God is and who I am in relationship with Him. At an immediate, "fleshed out" level, I saw what God is like in my husband—steadfast love, covenant faithfulness, kindness, reliability, full of grace and truth. I also saw God show Himself in the care of our church community, who provided an extended, stable family, helping our children transition back into an American culture.

When we returned to the United States from the Middle East, I felt like such a failure, raw and exposed. It was hard to open the door and let people see me for who I was. By God's grace, the church we entered was both biblical and filled with grace. We were accepted without question or expectation. I could weep through services, give voice to doubts, show up or not show up. Families in the church took our kids on hiking trips, brought them to soccer practice, and carpooled to school. I learned many important lessons there. But most of all, I learned that every marriage needs a loving, believing community.

In many ways, this was a midlife "pause" in joint ministry that God allowed us. It was a time to heal, to be strengthened and renewed. Henry was given a home assignment with our mission that took care of our needs. This was a turning point when Henry understood more deeply that God didn't love and value him because of how productive he was or because of his obedience and conformity to Scripture. God just loved him—as a father loves a son.

Patient counseling and community slowly brought healing. I had to relearn almost from the beginning what God is like. Over the years, my understanding of God had become overlaid with distortions. The God of my childhood dutifully loved me but didn't necessarily like me. He was someone who couldn't be counted on to intervene when bad things happened. In seminary, He had become the God of correct theology. In early marriage, He had been the sovereign God that required obedience at any cost. As we kept pace in the demands of ministry, He became the Engineer who ran a powerful machine. At its core, my depression was a consequence of mistrust in the character of God and a misunderstanding of His work and ways.

So step by step, God rebuilt my trust in His character. I deeply relearned about His steadfast love through the faithful care and covenantal love of my husband. Any normal husband might have chosen the path of divorce in those circumstances. But Henry modeled to me God's repeated words through all of Scripture, in all the circumstances of His people's unfaithfulness and fallenness: "I will never leave you nor forsake you" (Heb. 13:5). Henry's commitment to me didn't depend on how I acted, looked, or responded. He loved me when I was "dead in [my] trespasses and sins" (Eph. 2:1). This is the Christlike love that underlies Christian marriage. It is a love that endures because God's presence and promises endure.

What advantages has age given your marriage?

Trust develops over time. Each difficulty in earlier seasons built stepping-stones of faith that helped us through challenges in subsequent seasons. We are slowly learning not to exclaim in frustration, "Why is this happening?" but to prayerfully ask: "What are You wanting to teach us? How are You training us in righteousness?" Being able to trust in God's good character has made our current phase of ministry so much freer than it was before. In some ways we are busier than ever before. But we understand in new ways how Psalm 100:2 is possible: "Serve the LORD with gladness!" As we walk down cobblestone streets steeped in history, we look at each other in wonder that at an age when most retire, we are still given this privilege to serve together. Church growth is slow, there are many obstacles in the culture, and rumors of war loom on the horizon. But we are God's people, it is God's work, and He holds history in His hand.

What has your marriage been able to do because it is happy?

We currently live in a context in which the biblical model of marriage is considered outdated. Cohabitation is common, divorce is common, and children grow up without any pattern to follow. Our ministry has involved quite a bit of work with children and youth. We find that what young people notice the most is that we have a happy marriage. It has surprised me, the joy and hope it gives them: maybe a happy, lifelong marriage is possible. This has paved the way for many gospel conversations and opportunities.

Being partners in ministry has also, I think, doubled our effectiveness. We bring two sets of gifts to the equation. As we have learned to minister as a team, we allow the other person to fill in our weaknesses, and we lend our strength where it is needed.

What encouragement would you give to someone in an unhappy marriage?

The source of joy always has to be Christ Himself. Often, we can become unhappy because our partner doesn't meet our expectations. We have expected him or her to be the joy-giver. Find fellowship with other believers who can support and encourage you. There is no such thing as a marriage that isn't difficult at times, but my heart aches for those who are married to unbelievers or to those who are mired in sin or addictions. It is hard to not shift our gaze and try to "fix" our partner. It can be a real relief to accept that we are not responsible to change anyone else's heart. All we can do is look to our Savior to change our own hearts.

What is your favorite thing about being married?

The companionship, the sharing, the blessing of always having a partner and trusted friend. I love unspoken, shared humor, traveling adventures, and having a safe place to come home to.

11

Mystery

This mystery is profound,
and I am saying that it refers to Christ and the church.
—Ephesians 5:32

In Proverbs, a wise man confesses limits to his comprehension. This includes zoology, physics, and dating:

> Three things are too wonderful for me;
> four I do not understand:
> the way of an eagle in the sky,
> the way of a serpent on a rock,
> the way of a ship on the high seas,
> and the way of a man with a virgin. (30:18–19)

Have you ever felt that bewilderment? One mother told of meeting her future daughter-in-law for the first time at an event: "She stepped out of my son's beat-up, old pickup truck in pearls and heels, looking just gorgeous, and I just thought, 'How on earth did he do that?'" How does a young, inexperienced man with little money and wisdom talk a gifted young woman into a life partnership? It is a mystery. Something goes on that we cannot grasp but can only sense and see.

If there is mystery in dating, there is even more when we examine marriage. Paul, at the end of his section on marriage in Ephesians 5, comes to the end of human language and understanding, and confesses that marriage is a "profound" mystery!

When Scripture speaks of "mystery," it should not conjure up mental images of Hercule Poirot or Sherlock Holmes. A biblical mystery is not a crime to be solved or a frightening scenario to figure out. When Scripture speaks of a mystery, it is speaking of something hidden that is being shown to us—something that was secret that God is revealing. Our finite understanding is expanded as God shows us His mysteries. And marriage is one of these.

Part of the mystery is providence: how someone is brought to a specific spouse out of all the people in the world and becomes bound to that person in God's plan. We cannot explain it. But we can embrace and admire it. The very reality that God provides a particular person should make that person precious to his or her spouse. Martin Luther simply wrote, "I would not exchange Katie for France or Venice because God has given her to me."[1]

In this providential joining, John Chrysostom saw another mystery: the idea that God uses marriage to undo the divisions that sin brought into this world. It is the mystery of unifying strangers into the closest friends: "Having forbidden the marriage of kindred, [God] led us out unto strangers and drew them again to us. For since by this natural kindred it was not possible that they should be connected with us, he connected the whole anew by marriage, uniting together whole families by the single person of the bride, and mingling entire races with races."[2] That should sound familiar, because that is another small picture of the gospel, and what God's salvation does in bringing together people of "all tribes and peoples and languages" (Rev. 7:9). Marriage is not just the mystery of two people uniting but the joining of two families, sometimes two cultures and languages and more.

Another part of the mystery is how two people can be so much the same and yet so different. Both human, fallen, eternal-souled, redeemed, embodied. Some of these similarities can actually make marriage hard! And yet spouses are concurrently different: different personalities, backgrounds, and idiosyncrasies. Despite all this, Christian marriage enables two people to come together, be sanctified, and serve Jesus better together than they could apart.

Can we understand how? No, but we can see its effects. One is to "experience ever-deepening meaning. . . .To have meaning in your life is better than to have what you want, because you may neither know what you want, nor what you truly need. . . . Meaning signifies that you are in the right place."[3] God does promise to give us what we truly need, and though it may, as Isaac Watts observed, come in a way that nearly drives us to despair, it will come.[4] Often, what we need is provided through a happy marriage, and meaning is always included in that.

Another effect of the mystery of marriage is its humbling. Real mystery brings humility. When physicists look at the universe or chemists look at the atom, trying to push a little farther into God's vast known, something there, through its sheer greatness, humbles. Albert Einstein wrote about "a rapturous amazement at the harmony of natural law, which reveals an intelligence of such superiority that, compared with it," all the best thinking "is an utterly insignificant reflection."[5] We use and enjoy the natural world long before we understand it. Marriage is similar. When we look at the design of marriage, it is far beyond our understanding, but strangely still within our grasp. Just as salvation does not happen through human initiation, neither does a marriage that reflects that salvation. It is there for the taking, but in the taking, we are receiving God's gift, not crafting it ourselves. This should drive us to despair of our own efforts in themselves and make us run to God's mercy. Mystery levels pride: a happy marriage is not something that we manufacture in our own strength. If anyone has a happy marriage, it is God's doing. God started it, and God continues to provide for it, partly by giving the couple the tools to maintain it.

But knowledge of this mystery and our own limitations can stabilize, because God promises to keep everyone whom He calls to Himself. The love of the Father is the guarantee that Christian marriage can be blessed and happy even in this fallen world. Amy Carmichael wrote of Christian community, "There is no force strong enough to hold us together as a company, and animate all our doings, but this one force of Love; and so there is a constant attack upon the love without which we are sounding brass and tinkling cymbal."[6] That is certainly true of a marriage: we cannot hold ourselves together. Only the Lord's love is more than sufficient to keep us as a picture of His own love.

Marriage is a taste of something more full, perfect, and satisfying than we can conceptualize. Robert Browning hinted of that mystery as he wrote of his marriage to Elizabeth: "Your part my part / In life, for good and ill. / . . . The pain / Of finite hearts that yearn."[7] A happy marriage will have in itself a yearning for more—something infinite. Jonathan Edwards explains: "If we spend our lives in the pursuit of a temporal happiness: . . . Death will blow up all our hopes and expectations, and will put an end to our enjoyment of these things."[8] The joy of a happy marriage as an end will disappoint. As a means, though, it will bless and enrich on earth, and that blessing will reach fulfillment in glory.

Is part of the mystery love? Love is something that humans have pondered for millennia and still fail to adequately define. But we can see it and the mystery that it is in Christian marriage: the love that continues despite a spouse's knowledge of our failings; love that is for better or worse, for richer or poorer, in sickness and in health; a mystery that living day to day in the reality of Christian love has the power to change us far more than rules and rebuke. It is certainly a mystery that God decided to use imperfect human love to help us understand the great mystery of Christ and the church. Only God could take that earthly love and use it to demonstrate His love for us in Christ. Our marriages need God's definition and example of love; without that context, our love becomes self-referential, limited to affection, without the goal of enjoying and glorifying God.

How God loves our spouses through us is a mystery. We are so weak and sinful that it seems as though we could only hurt each other, not be a vehicle for expression of God's kindness and care. But just as we so often see the love of God for us in the love of His people, we see it even more in a Christian spouse as God redeems this closest relationship into a conduit for His own care and blessing.

It is also a mystery that God has given so many expressions of Christ's love for the church. Just as each human being has deep similarities to all other humans, yet is distinct and individual, so each Christian marriage has a fundamental similarity to others, as a picture of Christ's love for His people, yet is not a clone of some ideal human relationship. Perhaps this is because, as fallen and limited beings, we need countless expressions of the Real to teach us more fully what it looks like.

And perhaps the greatest part of the mystery that is marriage comes with eternity: only when we leave this realm and even the happiest of marriages will we fully know what love is. Only when we are glorified—no longer married or given in marriage—will we be able to love to our created capacity. The full presence of Love will obliterate the need for the picture. There will be no lost world that needs an example. Personhood will have found its purpose and fullest expression. There, no sinners will need help and support through this world. Perfectly sanctified and glorified, we will need no accountability. No threat will challenge full-orbed safety. There will be no passing along of the faith: the number of the elect will be complete, and they will all know the Lord (Jer. 31:34), and that knowledge will cover the earth (Hab. 2:14). Fruitfulness will be perfected and fully visible. The band of pilgrims that was our community will be home, with no need for encouragement along the way. Time will be a thing of the past. There will not even be mystery in relationship: we will know fully, even as we have been fully known. Worship will swallow everything else.

This is because marriage, for all its joy and blessing, is still a temporary picture of the permanent. Jonathan Edwards observed:

> God is the highest good of the reasonable creature. The enjoyment of Him is our proper happiness; and is the only happiness with which our souls can be satisfied. To go to heaven, to fully enjoy God, is infinitely better than the most pleasant accommodations

> here. Better than fathers and mothers, husbands, wives, or children. . . . These are but shadows; but the enjoyment of God is the substance. These are but scattered beams; but God is the sun. These are but streams; God is the fountain. These are but drops; God is the ocean.[9]

If we are Christians, we understand that this earth and its things are limited. We also know that God's best gifts—good in themselves—point to a higher good. So part of the mystery of marriage, which was made for us and given to us, is that it is not really about us. It is not even for us in the obvious ways that we might initially think. It was made for happiness, yes—the kind of deep happiness that springs from holiness because it is a deeper understanding of Jesus and His love for us. Martyn Lloyd-Jones wrote that "when we come to consider marriage, which is so common, and apparently so ordinary, we discover, if we are Christians, that we have to consider it in such a way that it brings us into the very centre of Christian truth, into the heart of theology and doctrine, into the mysteries of God in Christ as seen through the church."[10]

It is a mystery that marriage is so temporary but pictures something so eternal; a relationship so full of change but pictures something ultimately permanent; a union that consummation ends. So full of joy and blessing itself, marriage is only a dim picture of the joy and blessing that await us in Jesus. We do not do happy marriage ourselves. It is a gift that comes with the holiness that the Lord Himself provides in order to help us better understand our relationship with Him and to minister that love to a world that is in darkness.

Story (1964)

While the rest of the stories in this book follow a question-and-answer format, Judy preferred to write her answers in a more narrative form. She has lived in two different cultures within the United States, taught generations of college students, and served in several congregations. She currently lives with her family.

Widowhood is a sobering reality—sometimes it comes after years of loving care of an acutely ill husband, as in the passing of my first husband. Conversely, it can quickly intrude on a brief but devoted second marriage, as it did with my beloved husband Jim. In either situation, the intrusion is unwelcome and demands enormous adjustment. Decisions are required that are not only difficult but also jarring.

The familiar becomes strangely distant, and the reality of life without that dearly loved, God-ordained partner is no more. The evenings come altogether too soon. The nights are seemingly much longer than ever before. In the moments of restlessness in the middle of the night, one reaches across the bed to touch that warm body and realizes anew that he is not there.

The routine of breakfast, sharing thoughts from the Scriptures, and praying together as you start the day has come to an abrupt end. Oh, you know the Scriptures; you are cognizant of the many promises that have become so familiar over the years that they have become commonplace—promises like, "The effect of righteousness will be peace, and the result of righteousness, quietness and trust forever" (Isa. 32:17). The Holy Spirit reminds you that "the joy of the LORD will be your strength" (Neh. 8:10) and that "underneath are the everlasting arms" (Deut. 33:27). But right now you feel weak, vulnerable, and threatened.

In the new reality of loneliness and grief, suddenly one is keenly aware of the need for emotional and spiritual support—and that comes from the Scriptures and the loving concern of godly friends. In this hour of overwhelming need, several couples in our church with whom we had deeply established friendships very compassionately took me under their wing. They did not mother me or helicopter me, but instead they just invited me to join them for dinner occasionally or asked me to join them for a sandwich after church on Sunday evening. After my first husband's passing, one couple simply invited me for toast and jelly with tea after evening services. They could have served dry saltine crackers—the menu didn't matter. The fellowship was everything! Small things, perhaps, but these things brought joy to my heart in the midst of overwhelming loneliness.

At every turn, I urge older and younger couples alike to treasure every moment together. Marriage takes on an altogether new value when you no longer have a spouse.

I was widowed twice in six years. Both of my husbands were precious treasures to me. The first was a brilliant scientist and mathematician. We were "older" when we married: he was thirty-three, and

I was twenty-five. We were a team—the Lord blessed us with three wonderful children, and we had fifty years together and loved each other dearly. Both of us were believers before we married, so we had no conflicts there at all. I prayed that my dear husband would be a spiritual leader in our home, but that never happened. Nevertheless, by God's grace, we had a wonderful marriage.

Three years after the Lord took my first husband home following years of disabling health, I married my Sunday school teacher. Not everyone gets to do that! He was also a brilliant man: a theologian and historian. This was definitely a "marriage made in heaven." Although we had only a brief three and a half years together, ours was a deeply devoted love—the answer to my prayer for a spiritual leader. In some ways, his homegoing was much more difficult than the first.

But the Lord is faithful to His promises. With His help, I have survived the second experience of widowhood, during which the Lord sustained me and deserves all the credit for that. There are still long evenings and lonely nights on occasion, even after years, but I can give the Lord praise and glory for survival.

There are blessings, too! My walk with the Lord has been strengthened by widowhood. The Lord has taught me many lessons about trust and dependency. My devotional life is far deeper and more spiritually edifying than it ever was before. My desire to be in the Word and the satisfaction that I derive from that time is much more rewarding. My prayer life is much more intentional. These are just a few of the blessings that widowhood has afforded me.

The night before my second marriage, Jim and I prayed together that if the Lord would give us three months together, we would make the most of it, and if He gave us three years, we would serve Him every minute of it. Almost to the day, the Lord gave us three years and three months. We were a team. Loved each other dearly. Served the Lord to the best of our ability until the Lord took him home.

Eternity seems theoretical—almost ethereal—when one is married, busy with family and life. But eternity suddenly becomes reality when one loses a dearly loved spouse. That prayer book you used together becomes a treasure: full of memories of things shared; his poorly written, sparse notes that you found in it after he was gone; notes about death and, more importantly, about the resurrection (which dominated our conversation at every meal in his last weeks here). It was as though he knew that the end of his life was near: he taught me constantly from the Scriptures about the necessity of my future, full dependence on the Lord and His Word.

After three days in a deep coma, my beloved husband spoke two words in the presence of his three children and me: "God's grace." It amazed us all. The next day, the Lord took Jim home, but those two words remain in my memory—they characterized his life. He taught me so much: kind, gentlehearted, loving the Lord with every ounce of energy that he possessed, and loving me supremely.

Loneliness intrudes at times, but the precious memories of those last few years are constant reminders of a life well lived, a race well run, and a crown well won. Praise be to God!

12

Doxology

Every good gift and every perfect gift is from above,
coming down from the Father of lights, with whom
there is no variation or shadow due to change.
—James 1:17

This vision of Christian marriage may sound too good to be true. It would be, if it were something that we had dreamed up and had to work to fabricate for ourselves. But because marriage is a gift that pictures the bigger, truer, happier relationship of Christ and the church, we can embrace it as well as believe it and live it.

In her novel *Pride and Prejudice*, Jane Austen has Charlotte Lucas claim, "Happiness in marriage is entirely a matter of chance."[1] Lizzy rightly laughs at the idea. Acting on her conviction, Charlotte marries the silly Mr. Collins. Lizzy refuses to consider anyone whom she cannot truly respect. She has the advantage of understanding critical things about marriage from her parents' unhappy relationship, which saves her from making the same unhappy mistakes. But happiness in marriage is not a matter of chance, as though we were simply clever enough or lucky enough to make the right relational choice. For the Christian, happiness in marriage is due to God's design and His blessing on that design as two redeemed sinners seek to serve Him together. The unhappiness in marriage is our creation: disappointment so often is a result of putting our hope in another human. The happiness that we find in marriage is God's: most clear when our hope is in Him.

God is so good to give us the gift of marriage. He has linked holiness and happiness in the fabric of things, and His preserving grace means that obedience brings fulfillment and peace. Marriage becomes, for the believer, the context for deep joy and strength that God designed it to be—a growing up into Christ together. This will inescapably lead to happiness. It may come in fits and starts, in a two-steps-forward-one-step-back tempo, with roadblocks and darkness to overcome and bear, but it will be there and it will grow.

Marriage is bigger than our happiness, of course. Its purpose is beyond our own blessedness, from the care of children, to the stability of society, to the glory of God. But God did design happiness to go with marriage. He built in so many things to facilitate that joy. What a gift to take hold of. It is an incredible design that makes for deep blessing through this life.

This is why the expectation of happiness in a Christian marriage is a matter not of presumption but of faith. Everyone hopes for joy in personal relationships, but for so many, it is just a hope: "Some set out . . . with a glorious equipment of hope and enthusiasm, and get broken by the way, wanting patience with each other and the world."[2] This is Charlotte Collins' gamble. This is the chance of marriage without Christ. There is no recognition of design or direction or reality-giving meaning. Martin Bucer, preaching at the wedding of two young believers, explained why happiness is not chance for the Christian: "So, my dear friends, you must take it thoroughly to heart and not doubt that our dear God himself, by his special grace and compassion, has joined and united you to this everlasting happiness and well-being . . . bestowed for every good purpose. . . . You do not, however, belong to yourselves but belong to Jesus Christ, our Lord, who has purchased you with his blood unto a holy and blessed life."[3]

A happy marriage is not something that we manufacture, but this does not mean that it is easy. Jim Elliot commented that "marriage in God's view is intended to be an expensive thing."[4] Sometimes blessing comes through pain that we cannot predict or control. Creating happiness on our own is beyond us, as fallen and frail humans. A happy marriage, like faith itself, is a gift of God. If we are in a Christian marriage, we have the blessing of living under His blessing in this realm, and not His curse.

And it pictures the highest things—the eternal joy of Christ and His church. Martyn Lloyd-Jones called this comparison to marriage "the most exalted and wonderful statement [Paul] has ever made anywhere about the nature of the Christian church and her relationship to the Lord Jesus Christ."[5] While marriage enables us to better comprehend spiritual reality, the spiritual reality elevates our marriage, which will eventually be obliterated by the full spectacle of what it dimly reflected.

Christians must never love the picture—marriage—in isolation from what it pictures. If we love marriage apart from what it communicates and conveys, then that is idolatry. If we love marriage as a representation of Jesus' love, as the Father's good gift to His children, that is a love and appreciation that brings God glory.

When the Lord gives us marriage and teaches us to enjoy it in its right place, He also gives us happiness. It is a byproduct of the joy of salvation that gives our marriages exclusivity, closeness, and the rest. Like all other earthly happiness, marriage is both a preparation for and a foretaste of that full and perfect joy that awaits God's people, regardless of their relational status in this life. Again, Jonathan Edwards explains:

> We are designed for this future world. . . . God hath made us for himself. . . . There is but a very imperfect union with God to be had in this world. . . . Here we can serve and glorify God, but in an exceeding imperfect manner; our service being mingled with much sin and dishonor to God.
>
> But when we get to heaven (if ever that be), there we shall be brought to a perfect union with God. There we shall have clear views of God. We shall see face to face, and know as we are known. There we shall be fully conformed to God, without any remainder of sin. We shall be like him, for we shall see him as he is. There we shall serve God perfectly. . . . In heaven alone is the attainment of our highest good. God is the highest good of the reasonable creature. The enjoyment of him is our proper happiness; and is the only happiness with which our souls can be satisfied.[6]

Union with God—knowing fully even as we have been fully known—will dissolve all earthly relationships. This is why our joy in marriage is not a joy in the form itself, in the legal documents, the Mr. and Mrs., or any other external. Instead, it is the happiness of a relationship that all these externals point to and represent. As a representation of Jesus' love in this broken world, Christian marriage is not a way to show that we can create our own joy—a sort of "do this and live" when we cannot. Instead, it is an overflow of salvation lived out in the closest of human relationships. It is joyfully receiving Jesus' love through the love of another human being. Borrowing from eternity, Christian marriage brings the happiness of heaven down into this fallen world. The Giver of all good gifts gave us a very blessed one when He created marriage for our good and His glory. A believing couple can say with Bucer, "God has joined us together; he has helped us."[7]

Notes

Introduction

1 John Milton, *Paradise Lost*, in *The Student's Milton, Being the Complete Poems of John Milton with the Greater Part of His Prose Works* (New York: Appleton-Century-Crofts, 1933), 296.
2 Jane Austen, *Mansfield Park* (Ware, England: Wordsworth, 1992), 34.
3 *The Psalter: With Doctrinal Standards, Liturgy, Church Order, and Added Chorale Section* (Grand Rapids, Mich.: Eerdmans, 1999), 156.
4 "Two in the Campagna," in *The Complete Poetic and Dramatic Works of Robert Browning* (Boston: Houghton, Mifflin and Co., 1895), 189.
5 D. Martyn Lloyd-Jones, *Life in the Spirit in Marriage, Home, and Work: An Exposition of Ephesians 5:18 to 6:9* (Grand Rapids, Mich.: Baker, 1973), 140.
6 Augustine, *Confessions*, trans. Sarah Ruden (New York: Modern Library, 2017), 296.

Chapter 1

1 Jane Austen, *Sense and Sensibility* (Oxford, England: Oxford University Press, 2017), 191–92.
2 Jay L. Zagorsky, "Marriage and Divorce's Impact on Wealth," *Journal of Sociology* 41, no. 4, first published online June 30, 2016, https://journals.sagepub.com, accessed February 27, 2023.
3 Alexandra Sifferlin, "Do Married People Really Live Longer?," *Time*, February 12, 2015, https://time.com/3706692/do-married-people-really-live-longer/, accessed February 27, 2023.
4 J. I. Packer, *Knowing God* (Downers Grove, Ill.: InterVarsity Press, 1993), 126.
5 Lady Pamela Hicks, *Daughter of Empire: My Life as a Mountbatten* (New York: Simon and Schuster, 2012), 5.

6 Hicks, *Daughter of Empire*, 24.
7 John Chrysostom, "Homily 6," in *The Nicene and Post-Nicene Fathers of the Christian Church*, ed. Philip Schaff, 1st ser. (Grand Rapids, Mich.: Eerdmans, 1986), 10:42.
8 John Newton, "Glorious Things of Thee Are Spoken" (1779), in *Trinity Hymnal* (Suwanee, Ga.: Great Commission, 1990), no. 345.
9 Chalmers preached to his Scottish congregation on 1 John 2:15, giving the sermon this title. It was later published as a small book and is still in print today.
10 Sinclair B. Ferguson, *Love Came Down at Christmas* ([Epsom, England]: Good Book, 2018), 71.
11 Albert Einstein, *Ideas and Opinions* (New York: Modern Library, 1994), 53. Despite these sorts of insights, Einstein was unable to live up to them, living with his wife as though his needs and desires mattered the most, forcing her into subservience to his wants in a dysfunctional marriage.
12 Benjamin Franklin, *Poor Richard's Almanac* (Philadelphia: B. Franklin at the New Printing Office, 1739), n.p.
13 Anna L. Waring, "Father, I Know That All My Life" (1850), in *Trinity Hymnal*, no. 559.
14 Austen, *Mansfield Park*, 336.
15 David Gibson, "Your Significance Is in Your Servitude," sermon preached at Trinity Church, Aberdeen, Scotland, December 4, 2022.
16 Milton, *Paradise Lost*, in *The Student's Milton*, 294.
17 *The Journals of Jim Elliot: Missionary, Martyr, Man of God*, ed. Elisabeth Elliot (Grand Rapids, Mich.: Baker, 2020), 395.

Chapter 2

1 Martin Bucer, quoted in H.J. Selderhuis, *Marriage and Divorce in the Thought of Martin Bucer*, trans. John Vriend and Lyle D. Bierma (Kirksville, Mo.: Thomas Jefferson University Press, 1999), 168.
2 Jordan B. Peterson, *12 Rules for Life: An Antidote to Chaos* (Toronto: Random House, 2018), 271.
3 "The Woodpile," in *Complete Poems of Robert Frost* (New York: Holt, Rinehart and Winston, 1964), 127.
4 *Julius Caesar*, act 2, sc. 1, in *The Complete Works of William Shakespeare* (New York: Nelson Doubleday, n.d.), 2:579.
5 Anne Brontë, *Agnes Grey* (New York: Penguin, 1988), 155.

6 Alfred, Lord Tennyson, "Locksley Hall," in *Harvard Classics: English Poetry* (New York: P.F. Collier & Son Co., 1938), 3:980.
7 Martin Luther, quoted in Roland Bainton, *Here I Stand* (New York: Abingdon, 1950), 301.
8 C.S. Lewis, *The Four Loves* (New York: Harper Collins, 1960), 155.
9 Luther, quoted in Bainton, *Here I Stand*, 290.
10 Dorothy Canfield, preface to *The Home-Maker* (Thorndike, Maine: Center Point, n.d.), 10.
11 Lloyd-Jones, *Life in the Spirit in Marriage, Home, and Work*, 223.
12 Lloyd-Jones, *Life in the Spirit in Marriage, Home, and Work*, 226.
13 J.C. Pollock, *Hudson Taylor and Maria: Pioneers in China* (New York: McGraw-Hill, 1962), 102.
14 Amelia Karraker and Kenzie Latham, "In Sickness and in Health? Physical Illness as a Risk Factor for Marital Dissolution in Later Life," *Journal of Health and Social Behavior* 56, no. 3 (September 2015): 420–35. While the authors focus on the fifty-plus demographic, the paper also references studies showing similar trends in younger couples.
15 Milton, *Paradise Lost*, in *The Student's Milton*, 294.
16 Bucer, quoted in Selderhuis, *Marriage and Divorce*, 173.
17 Tim Keller, *The Meaning of Marriage: Facing the Complexities of Commitment with the Wisdom of God* (2011; repr., New York: Penguin, 2016), 135.
18 Jay E. Adams, *Christian Living in the Home* (Phillipsburg, N.J.: P&R, 1972), 13.

Chapter 3

1 Jane Austen, *Pride and Prejudice* (New York: Barnes & Noble, 1993), 31.
2 John Owen, *The Holy Spirit* (Edinburgh, Scotland: Banner of Truth, 2021), 231.
3 Jack Fishman, *My Darling Clementine: The Story of Lady Churchill* (New York: David McKay, 1963), 57.
4 T.S. Eliot, "The Wasteland," in *The Norton Anthology of English Literature*, ed. M.H. Abrams (New York: W.W. Norton & Co., 1975), 2532.

Chapter 4

1 "Solemnization of Matrimony," in *The Book of Common Prayer 1959 Canada* (Toronto: Anglican Book Centre, n.d.), 564.

2 John Chrysostom, "Homily 34," in *The Nicene and Post-Nicene Fathers of the Christian Church*, ed. Philip Schaff, 1st ser. (Grand Rapids, Mich.: Eerdmans, 1989), 12:204.
3 *Letters of William Still* (Edinburgh, Scotland: Banner of Truth, 1984), 166.
4 *Letters of William Still*, 166.
5 *Letters of William Still*, 167, brackets original.

Chapter 5

1 *The Journals of Jim Elliot*, 217.
2 Bucer, quoted in Selderhuis, *Marriage and Divorce*, 186.
3 Peterson, *12 Rules for Life*, 272–73.
4 Peterson, *12 Rules for Life*, 275.
5 Amy Carmichael, *If* (Grand Rapids, Mich.: Zondervan, 1965), n.p.
6 Carmichael, *If*, n.p.
7 Elisabeth Elliot, "The Taking of Human Life". *The Elisabeth Elliot Newsletter*, March/April 1983, 1, elisabethelliot.org, accessed January 27, 2025.
8 Bucer, quoted in Roland Bainton, *Women of the Reformation in Germany and Italy* (Minneapolis: Augsburg, 1971), 88.
9 Martin Greschat, *Martin Bucer: A Reformer and His Times*, trans. Stephen E. Buckwalter (Louisville, Ky.: Westminster John Knox, 2004), 141.

Chapter 6

1 Luther, quoted in Bainton, *Here I Stand*, 287.
2 Matthew Henry, *The NIV Matthew Henry Commentary in One Volume*, ed. Leslie F. Church (Grand Rapids, Mich.: Zondervan, 1992), 7.
3 *The Journals of Jim Elliot*, 354.
4 Henry Baskerville Walton, ed., *The First Book of Common Prayer of Edward VI, and the Ordinal of 1549, Together with the Order of the Communion, 1548* (London: Rivingtons, 1869), n.p.
5 John Milton, "Christian Doctrine," in *The Student's Milton*, 1048.
6 U.S. Surgeon General, *Our Epidemic of Loneliness and Isolation: The U.S. Surgeon General's Advisory on the Healing Effects of Social Connection and Community* (Washington, D.C.: Public Health Service, 2023), https://www.hhs.gov/sites/default/files/surgeon-general-social-connection-advisory.pdf, accessed December 29, 2023. Eighty-two pages detail the

multifaceted effects on individuals and society. The prevalence of one-person households is rising in the West, showing and perpetuating the foolishness of abandoning God's design.

7 Married people, though, are statistically wealthier and more financially stable than their unmarried peers. Brad Wilcox, "Two Is Wealthier than One: Marital Status and Wealth Outcomes among Preretirement Adults," *The Institute For Family Studies*, December 1, 2021, accessed January 23, 2025.

Chapter 7

1 Einstein, *Ideas and Opinions*, 52.

2 Katharina Schutz-Zell, "Apologia for Master Matthew Zell, Her Husband, Who Is Pastor and Servant of the Word in Strasbourg . . . ," in *Church Mother: The Writings of a Protestant Reformer in Sixteenth-Century Germany*, ed. and trans. Elise McKee (Chicago: University of Chicago Press, 2006), 79.

Chapter 8

1 Bucer, quoted in Selderhuis, *Marriage and Divorce*, 171.

2 Sinclair B. Ferguson, *Maturity: Growing Up and Going On in the Christian Life* (Edinburgh, Scotland: Banner of Truth, 2019), 16.

Chapter 9

1 Elisabeth Elliot, "The Taking of Human Life," 1.

2 Johann Franck, "Soul, Adorn Yourself with Gladness" (1649), in *Trinity Psalter Hymnal* (Willow Grove, Pa.: OPC/URC, 2021), no. 200

3 Sinclair B. Ferguson, *Devoted to God's Church* (Edinburgh, Scotland: Banner of Truth, 2020), 66–67.

4 Ferguson, *Maturity*, 28.

5 Charles Spurgeon, *Lectures to My Students* (Pasadena, Tex.: Pilgrim, 1990), 2:12.

6 Sinclair B. Ferguson, *Worthy: Living in Light of the Gospel* (Wheaton, Ill.: Crossway, 2023), 60.

7 Packer, *Knowing God*, 123.

8 J. Franck, "Deck Thyself, My Soul, with Gladness" (1649), in *The Lutheran Hymnary* (Minneapolis: Augsburg, 1935), 149.

9 Packer, *Knowing God*, 216.

10 "The Armful," in *Complete Poems of Robert Frost*, 343.

11 Owen, *The Holy Spirit*, 173.
12 Owen, *The Holy Spirit*, 156.
13 Bernard of Clairvaux, "Jesus, Thou Joy of Loving Hearts" (c. 1150), in *Trinity Hymnal*, no. 646.

Chapter 10

1 John Archibald Wheeler with Kenneth Ford, *Geons, Black Holes, and Quantum Foam: A Life in Physics* (New York: Norton, 2000), 235.
2 As part of creation, *chronos* does not exist in eternity where God dwells (Isa. 57:15). His promises and purposes are outside time (Titus 1:2), and so will humanity be at the end of time, in either heaven or hell.
3 James W. Pennebaker, *The Secret Life of Pronouns: What Our Words Say about Us* (New York: Bloomsbury, 2011), 232–33.
4 "Any Wife to Any Husband," in *The Complete Poetic and Dramatic Works of Robert Browning*, 188.
5 David Kheridan, *The Road from Home: The Story of an Armenian Girl* (New York: Beech Tree, 1979), 144.
6 Pennebaker, *Secret Life of Pronouns*, 129.
7 Ferguson, *Maturity*, 3.
8 Anthony Trollope, *The Small House at Allington* (London: Oxford University Press, 1959), 42.
9 Austen, *Mansfield Park*, 332.
10 Charles Dickens, "Sketches of Young Couples," in *Sketches by Boz: Illustrative of Everyday Life and Everyday People* (London: J.M. Dent, 1931), 536.
11 Jane Austen, *Persuasion* (Edinburgh, Scotland: John Grant, 1905), 356.
12 Hannah Flagg Gould, "Aged Saint," Challies.com (blog), April 2, 2023, accessed April 2, 2023.
13 Elizabeth Gaskell, *Wives and Daughters* (New York: Penguin, 1996), 255.
14 Augustine, *Confessions*, 164. Before his conversion, Augustine had lived with his mistress for many years in what we would call a common-law relationship. Though the two had a son together, loved each other, were both converted, and could have married each other with no obstacle from Roman or biblical law, Augustine's godly mother had social ambitions for her son that excluded this woman, and she was sent away. She joined a convent in North Africa and never saw Augustine or their son again.

15 Caroline M. Noel, "To S. N.," in *The Name of Jesus, and Other Poems for the Sick and Lonely* (London: Hatchards, 1876), n.p.
16 James Stalker, *Imago Christi: The Example of Jesus Christ* (London: Hodder & Stoughton, 1894), 107.

Chapter 11

1 Luther, quoted in Bainton, *Here I Stand*, 288.
2 John Chrysostom, "Homily XXX on Matt IX.9," in *The Nicene and Post-Nicene Fathers of the Christian Church*, ed. Philip Schaff, 1st ser. (Grand Rapids, Mich.: Eerdmans, 1986), 10:204–5.
3 Peterson, *12 Rules for Life*, 200.
4 Isaac Watts, "Prayer Answered by Crosses" in *The Psalms, Hymns and Spiritual Songs of the Rev. Isaac Watts, D. D.*, edited by Samuel Worchester (Boston, Mass: Crocker and Brewster, 1842), 540–541.
5 Einstein, *Ideas and Opinions*, 43.
6 Carmichael, *If*, n.p.
7 "Two in the Campagna," in *The Complete Poetic and Dramatic Works of Robert Browning*, 189.
8 Jonathan Edwards, "The True Christian's Life a Journey towards Heaven," in *The Works of President Edwards* (New York: Leavitt & Allen, 1852), 4:575.
9 Edwards, *The Works of President Edwards*, 4:575.
10 Lloyd-Jones, *Life in the Spirit in Marriage, Home, and Work*, 141.

Chapter 12

1 Austen, *Pride and Prejudice*, 16.
2 George Eliot, *Middlemarch* (New York: Penguin, 1994), 832.
3 Bucer, quoted in Selderhuis, *Marriage and Divorce*, 220.
4 November 1, 1949, in *The Journals of Jim Elliot*, 176.
5 Lloyd-Jones, *Life in the Spirit in Marriage, Home, and Work*, 130.
6 Edwards, *The Works of President Edwards, 4:575.*
7 Bucer, quoted in Selderhuis, *Marriage and Divorce*, 62.

Bibliography

Very often, the best books on marriage are not marriage books. This collection of titles comprises works that were not addressed to couples asking questions about their union but that strongly influenced this book because they spoke to an aspect of life, godliness, or relationship that directly affects a marriage and its happiness.

Alfred, Lord Tennyson. "Locksley Hall." In *Harvard Classics: English Poetry*, vol. III, 979–86. New York: P.F. Collier & Son Co., 1938.

Augustine. *Confessions*. Translated by Sarah Ruden. New York: Modern Library, 2017.

Austen, Jane. *Mansfield Park*. Ware, England: Wordsworth, 1992.

———. *Persuasion*. Edinburgh, Scotland: John Grant, 1905.

———. *Pride and Prejudice*. New York: Barnes & Noble, 1993.

———. *Sense and Sensibility*. Oxford, England: Oxford University Press, 2017.

Bainton, Roland. *Here I Stand*. New York: Abingdon, 1950.

———. *Women of the Reformation in Germany and Italy*. Minneapolis: Augsburg, 1971.

The Book of Common Prayer 1959 Canada. Toronto: Anglican Book Centre, n.d.

Brontë, Anne. *Agnes Grey*. New York: Penguin, 1988.

Browning, Robert. *The Complete Poetic and Dramatic Works of Robert Browning*. Boston: Houghton, Mifflin and Co., 1895.

Canfield, Dorothy. *The Home-Maker*. Thorndike, Maine: Center Point, n.d.

Carmichael, Amy. *If*. Grand Rapids, Mich.: Zondervan, 1965.

Chrysostom, John. *Homilies*. In *The Nicene and Post-Nicene Fathers of the Christian Church*, 1st series, vols. 10 and 12. Edited by Philip Schaff. Grand Rapids, Mich.: Eerdmans, 1986 and 1989.

Dickens, Charles. *Sketches by Boz: Illustrative of Everyday Life and Everyday People*. London: J.M. Dent, 1931.

Edwards, Jonathan. *The Works of President Edwards*. New York: Leavitt & Allen, 1852.

Einstein, Albert. *Ideas and Opinions*. New York: Modern Library, 1994.

Eliot, George. *Middlemarch*. New York: Penguin, 1994.

Eliot, T.S. "The Wasteland." In *The Norton Anthology of English Literature*, edited by M.H. Abrams, 2527–43. New York: W.W. Norton & Co., 1975.

Elliot, Elisabeth. "The Taking of Human Life." *The Elisabeth Elliot Newsletter*, March/April 1983, 1–2. elisabethelliot.org. Accessed January 27, 2025.

Elliot, Jim. *The Journals of Jim Elliot: Missionary, Martyr, Man of God*. Edited by Elisabeth Elliot. Grand Rapids, Mich.: Baker, 2020.

Ferguson, Sinclair B. *Devoted to God's Church*. Edinburgh, Scotland: Banner of Truth, 2020.

———. *Love Came Down at Christmas*. [Epsom, England]: Good Book, 2018.

———. *Maturity: Growing Up and Going On in the Christian Life*. Edinburgh, Scotland: Banner of Truth, 2019.

———. *Worthy: Living in Light of the Gospel*. Wheaton, Ill.: Crossway, 2023.

Fishman, Jack. *My Darling Clementine: The Story of Lady Churchill*. New York: David McKay, 1963.

Franklin, Benjamin. *Poor Richard's Almanac*. Philadelphia: B. Franklin at the New Printing Office, 1739.

Frost, Robert. *Complete Poems of Robert Frost*. New York: Holt, Rinehart and Winston, 1964.

Gaskell, Elizabeth. *Wives and Daughters*. New York: Penguin, 1996.

Gibson, David. "Your Significance Is in Your Servitude." Sermon preached at Trinity Church, Aberdeen, Scotland, December 4, 2022.

Greschat, Martin. *Martin Bucer: A Reformer and His Times*. Translated by Stephen E. Buckwalter. Louisville, Ky.: Westminster John Knox, 2004.

Hicks, Lady Pamela. *Daughter of Empire: My Life as a Mountbatten*. New York: Simon and Schuster, 2012.

Henry, Matthew. *The NIV Matthew Henry Commentary in One Volume*. Edited by Leslie F. Church. Grand Rapids, Mich: Zondervan, 1992.

Karraker, Amelia, and Kenzie Latham. "In Sickness and in Health? Physical Illness as a Risk Factor for Marital Dissolution in Later Life." *Journal of Health and Social Behavior* 56, no. 3 (September 2015): 420–35.

Kheridan, David. *The Road from Home: The Story of an Armenian Girl*. New York: Beech Tree, 1979.

Lewis, C.S. *The Four Loves*. New York: Harper Collins, 1960.

Lloyd-Jones, D. Martyn. *Life in the Spirit in Marriage, Home, and Work: An Exposition of Ephesians 5:18 to 6:9*. Grand Rapids, Mich.: Baker, 1973.

The Lutheran Hymnary. Minneapolis: Augsburg, 1935.

Milton, John. *The Student's Milton, Being the Complete Poems of John Milton with the Greater Part of His Prose Works*. New York: Appleton-Century-Crofts, 1933.

Noel, Caroline M. *The Name of Jesus, and Other Poems for the Sick and Lonely*. London: Hatchards, 1876.

Owen, John. *The Holy Spirit*. Edinburgh, Scotland: Banner of Truth, 2021.

Packer, J.I. *Knowing God*. Downers Grove, Ill.: InterVarsity Press, 1993.

Pennebaker, James W. *The Secret Life of Pronouns: What Our Words Say about Us*. New York: Bloomsbury, 2011.

Peterson, Jordan B. *12 Rules for Life: An Antidote to Chaos*. Toronto: Random House, 2018.

Pollock, J.C. *Hudson Taylor and Maria: Pioneers in China*. New York: McGraw-Hill, 1962.

The Psalter: With Doctrinal Standards, Liturgy, Church Order, and Added Chorale Section. Grand Rapids, Mich.: Eerdmans, 1999.

Schutz-Zell, Katharina. *Church Mother: The Writings of a Protestant Reformer in Sixteenth-Century Germany*. Edited and translated by Elise McKee. Chicago: University of Chicago Press, 2006.

Selderhuis, H.J. *Marriage and Divorce in the Thought of Martin Bucer*. Translated by John Vriend and Lyle D. Bierma. Kirksville, Mo.: Thomas Jefferson University Press, 1999.

Shakespeare, William. *The Complete Works of William Shakespeare*. New York: Nelson Doubleday, n.d.

Sifferlin, Alexandra. "Do Married People Really Live Longer?" *TIME*, February 12, 2015. https://time.com/3706692/do-married-people-really-live-longer/. Accessed February 27, 2023.

Spurgeon, Charles. *Lectures to My Students*. 4 vols. in 1. Pasadena, Tex.: Pilgrim, 1990.

Stalker, James. *Imago Christi: The Example of Jesus Christ*. London: Hodder & Stoughton, 1894.

Still, William. *Letters of William Still*. Edinburgh, Scotland: Banner of Truth, 1984.

Trinity Hymnal. Suwanee, Ga.: Great Commission, 1990.

Trinity Psalter Hymnal. Willow Grove, Pa.: OPC/URC, 2021.

Trollope, Anthony. *The Small House at Allington*. London: Oxford University Press, 1959.

U.S. Surgeon General. *Our Epidemic of Loneliness and Isolation: The U.S. Surgeon General's Advisory on the Healing Effects of Social Connection and Community*. Washington, D.C.: Public Health Service, 2023. https://www.hhs.gov/sites/default/files/surgeon-general-social-connection-advisory.pdf. Accessed December 29, 2023.

Walton, Henry Baskerville, ed. *The First Book of Common Prayer of Edward VI, and the Ordinal of 1549, Together with the Order of the Communion, 1548*. London: Rivingtons, 1869.

Watts, Isaac. *The Psalms, Hymns and Spiritual Songs of the Rev. Isaac Watts, D. D.*. Edited by Samuel Worchester Boston, Mass: Crocker and Brewster, 1842.

Wheeler, John Archibald, with Kenneth Ford. *Geons, Black Holes, and Quantum Foam: A Life in Physics*. New York: Norton, 2000.

Wilcox, Brad. "Two is Wealthier Than One: Marital Status and Wealth Outcomes Among Preretirement Adults" in *The Institute For Family Studies*. First published online December 1, 2021. Accessed January 23, 2025

Zagorsky, Jay L. "Marriage and Divorce's Impact on Wealth." *Journal of Sociology* 41, no. 4. First published online June 30, 2016. https://journals.sagepub.com. Accessed February 27, 2023.

Subject Index

About the Author

Rebecca VanDoodewaard is a wife, mother, pastor's daughter, and author. Living in view of the Appalachians, she spends her time teaching her children, learning in her local church, and hosting people in her home alongside her husband, a church history professor. Her books include *Reformation Women: Sixteenth-Century Women Who Shaped Christianity's Rebirth* and the Banner Board Books series for children.